Funny Business

A Comedy

Derek Benfield

A SAMUEL FRENCH ACTING EDITION

FOUNDED 1830

SAMUELFRENCH-LONDON.CO.UK
SAMUELFRENCH.COM

FOR AMATEUR PRODUCTION ENQUIRIES

UNITED KINGDOM AND WORLD EXCLUDING NORTH AMERICA

plays@SamuelFrench-London.co.uk

020 7255 4302/01

Each title is subject to availability from Samuel French,

depending upon country of performance.

FUNNY BUSINESS

First produced by Sally Hughes at The Mill at Sonning Dinner Theatre on 25th June 2002, with the following cast:

Ferris	Richard Buss
Henry	Martyn Stanbridge
Angela	Elizabeth Elvin
Judy	Belinda Carroll
Mr Johnson	Barrie Gosney
Edgar	Timothy Carlton

Directed by Ian Masters

Setting by Emily Cross

ACT I

A small unfashionable hotel in the depths of the country. A Friday evening in Summer

A modest entrance hall with an untidy reception desk above which is an archway leading to the main entrance and the garden. The first few steps of two staircases, one leading up and off L and the other up and off R. There is a way off to the kitchen DR, and a door to the lounge DL, above which is a small cupboard. A dilapidated sofa is L with a coffee table on its right and a potted plant on a tray on the floor to its left. A drinks trolley is R. There are two bedrooms, one L decorated blue and one R decorated pink, which are raised above the level of the reception area. Each bedroom has a door to the corridor and another to the bathroom. The lighting in the reception area will remain on throughout, whereas the lights in the bedrooms will come on and off as required. Music before the play will stop when the Lights come up in the reception area

Someone is asleep, lying on the sofa, feet hanging over one end, face covered by a newspaper. Snoring, possibly. Not a worry in the world. For a few moments nothing happens. We begin to wonder if anything is ever going to happen...

Then the reception phone rings abruptly. The recumbent figure cries out in surprise, and falls off the sofa, clutching at the newspaper that was hiding his face

Ferris Aaaah!!

Ferris is a mischievous, somewhat disreputable man in his fifties. He struggles to his feet and ambles sleepily across to the phone to lift the receiver

(*Yawning, wearily*) Yes? Hullo? (*He hastily gathers himself*) Oh, it's *you*! ... What? (*Outraged*) Of *course* I wasn't asleep! I'm far too busy to be asleep! What do you want, anyway? (*He listens*) Coming *here*? Who's coming here? (*With increasing anxiety*) Oh, no—no—I can't deal with that sort of thing! *You* should be here to deal with that sort of thing. (*A beat*) I know you're not here! You're *there*, and *I*'m here! That's the trouble.

(*Reluctantly*) Oh, all right, then, if I have to. What's his name? (*Unable to hear*) What? I can't hear you! Don't go away! (*He lowers the receiver and looks up*) She's gone away... (*He hangs up*) Oh, my God!

Henry comes in from the main entrance. He is a shy, middle-aged man in a bit of a state

Henry Has she arrived?
Ferris (*belligerently*) Of course she hasn't arrived!
Henry She said she'd be here by six.
Ferris She's not due back until Thursday.
Henry (*appalled*) Thursday?!
Ferris Well, she went for ten days, and ten days isn't up until Thursday. That was her on the phone!
Henry What are you talking about?
Ferris My sister. Isn't that who you meant?
Henry No! I'm not interested in your sister!

Ferris is rather offended by this apparent slight on his sister

Ferris You might be, wait till you *see* her before you pass judgement.
Henry But I'm already spoken for.
Ferris You'd be wasting your time, anyway. She's in Benidorm.
Henry Benidorm?
Ferris She got fed up with going to Frinton, so this year she decided to take the plunge and go to Benidorm. I'm holding the fort in her absence.
Henry I must have written to *her*, then?
Ferris In *Benidorm*?
Henry In this hotel!
Ferris You mean you've been corresponding with my sister? You said you weren't interested in her.
Henry To make the booking!
Ferris You mean you're *coming* here?
Henry Of course I'm coming here! I've already arrived, haven't I? Don't you remember? You showed me to my room.
Ferris Did I? I never can remember faces.
Henry This afternoon! I checked in this afternoon!
Ferris Oh, well, that explains it. I'm never at my best after lunch. (*With a sudden thought*) Wait a minute! What are you coming here *for*?
Henry (*guiltily*) N-n-nothing...! (*He backs away*)
Ferris Coming here for n-n-nothing?
Henry I—I don't want to talk about it...

Ferris jumps to the obvious conclusion

Ferris Ah! It's *you*, isn't it?
Henry (*puzzled*) Sorry?

Ferris gives a big, welcoming smile and goes to him, assuming an air of extreme servility

Ferris Oh, sir! You should have said! I'd have had the champagne and caviar out to welcome you.
Henry What *are* you talking about?
Ferris You're a journalist! You write for a Sunday newspaper!
Henry No!
Ferris No?
Henry No!
Ferris Oh… Well, what *are* you here for, then?
Henry N-n-nothing…
Ferris Well, let's see which room you're going to do n-n-nothing in, shall we? (*He goes to get the register*)
Henry I'm in the honeymoon suite.

Ferris holds his look, then laughs at the idea

Ferris You're not, are you?
Henry Yes. I am!

Ferris gives him the once-over

Ferris You don't look like a newly-wed to me.
Henry (*embarrassed*) No. I'm not.
Ferris I see. Just reminiscing. Does *she* know? That you're in the honeymoon suite?
Henry Of course she knows! She made the booking, didn't she?
Ferris Not my sister! The one you're expecting. You are expecting someone, aren't you?
Henry Yes… (*Then, defensively*) We're here on business!
Ferris And we know what *sort* of business, don't we? (*He laughs raucously*)
Henry Now look here, Mr Ferris—you're supposed to be discreet. That's what it said in your advertisement. It said discretion was your speciality.

Ferris grins cheekily

Ferris You've got something to hide, haven't you?
Henry No…
Ferris Yes, you have! Discretion wouldn't be required if your relationship

was above board, now would it? (*He nudges him playfully*) You should
know better than this at your age! (*He laughs*)

Henry You ... you will keep it under your hat, won't you?

Ferris I don't know about that, sir. This is a respectable hotel. (*He holds out
his hand hopefully*)

Henry passes him some money

It's under my hat. This your first time for some time, is it?

Henry Well ... in a way.

Ferris First time with somebody else's wife, eh? (*He laughs again*)

Henry (*unhappily*) If she turns up. She should have been here by now. I'll
go upstairs and wait for her there, shall I?

Ferris Good idea. You have a rest while you've got the chance. I'll send her
up to you as soon as she arrives.

Henry (*gratefully*) Oh, thank you, Ferris.

Ferris Thank *you*, sir. (*He holds out his hand pointedly*)

*Henry reluctantly gives him some more money. Ferris pretends to be
surprised*

Oh, that *is* kind, sir! Very kind indeed. You didn't have to do that again.
My sister says we're not supposed to accept tips.

Henry Oh—sorry.

Henry makes to retrieve the money, but Ferris hastily pockets it

Ferris But I'll make an exception in your case.

Not best pleased, Henry goes out up the R stairs

*Ferris goes to the desk and takes out a notice which he places prominently
on the desk. The notice reads "NO VACANCIES"*

*Angela, a confident, attractive business lady in her 40s strides in from the
main entrance, carrying a weekend bag*

Ferris sees her—and jumps to conclusions

Well! About time, too! You've just missed him.

Naturally, Angela is surprised by such a reception

Angela Who the hell are you?

Ferris Mr Ferris! The deputy manager. *You* should have been here at six!
Angela Why? What happened?
Ferris Nothing happened, did it? You weren't here, so nothing *could* happen!
Angela Sorry?
Ferris You were expected by six! (*He points to his wristwatch*) And it's after six *now*, isn't it?
Angela I was held up.
Ferris Then you should have telephoned!
Angela I was on a train!
Ferris Didn't you have your mobile with you? Then I could have put him out of his misery. I'll tell you one thing—you're a bit younger than I expected!
Angela (*puzzled*) What *are* you talking about?

Ferris nudges her playfully

Ferris You don't have to pretend! Discretion is our middle name. Well, my sister's, that is. And I carry the banner of discretion in her absence. Benidorm. You ever been there?
Angela Benidorm?
Ferris Yes.
Angela No.
Ferris What?
Angela No. I've never been there!
Ferris Well, that's where my sister is. So I'm filling in here while she's on holiday. (*Playfully*) You should have said the magic words right away.
Angela What magic words?

Ferris glances around to make sure nobody is listening, then whispers, inaudibly

Ferris Honeymoon suite...
Angela I can't hear you!
Ferris It's supposed to be a secret! And it won't be a secret if I start yelling it all over the place, will it?
Angela But there's nobody else here! Surely you can say it a *little* louder?

Another look around before Ferris speaks with a little more volume

Ferris Honeymoon suite... (*He nods encouragingly, grinning the while*)

Angela hears it this time, and reacts loudly

Angela The *honeymoon* suite?!

Ferris quickly tries to silence her

Ferris Ssh! Ssh! You don't want everyone to hear, do you?
Angela Why should I want the honeymoon suite?
Ferris Surely you don't have to ask!
Angela But *I* haven't just got married.
Ferris Neither has he, but that doesn't matter, does it? (*He laughs coarsely*)

Angela tries to be patient

Angela Mr Ferris—watch my lips. I did not—repeat not—book the honeymoon suite.
Ferris No, of course *you* didn't! You didn't have to, did you? He did it *for* you. (*He nudges her playfully*) I wouldn't hang about if I were you. Don't want to waste any *more* time, do we?
Angela (*severely*) I do not wish to occupy the honeymoon suite! All right?
Ferris Well, you've got no choice, have you? See? (*He indicates the "NO VACANCIES" sign*) We're fully booked.

She looks at the sign dispiritedly

Oh, go on—you'll like it! It's got a four-poster. With a lovely view of the ceiling.
Angela Are you telling me there's no other room available?
Ferris (*indicating the sign again*) Well, that's what it says, doesn't it?
Angela (*with a sigh*) Oh, very well. I suppose, it'll have to do. (*She picks up her weekend bag*)
Ferris I'll take that, miss.
Angela No, you won't. (*She clutches it to her protectively*)
Ferris But I'm the acting manager! It's what I'm supposed to do.
Angela Well, you're not doing it with me!
Ferris Please yourself.
Angela Well, come on, then—give it to me!
Ferris Sorry?
Angela The key! The key! (*She holds out her hand*)
Ferris (*grinning*) Oh, you don't have to bother about a key. I think he'll let you in. The stairs to the right. Number Four, you can't miss it.
Angela (*coldly*) Thank you.
Ferris Thank *you*, miss. (*He holds out his hand hopefully*)

Puzzled, Angela shakes his hand formally and goes out up the R stairs

Ferris is unimpressed

I hope she's more generous in the boudoir...

Ferris goes out into the kitchen

Lights up in the Pink Room. There is indeed a four-poster, though not quite as glamorous as one might have hoped

Angela comes in, looking about uncertainly

Henry comes in from the bathroom excitedly, talking as he arrives

Henry Oh, good! You're here at last! (*He stops in his tracks, seeing a strange lady in his bedroom*) Who are you?
Angela Isn't it a bit late in the day to be cleaning the bathroom?
Henry I wasn't cleaning the bathroom!
Angela You mean you're not a member of staff?
Henry Of course I'm not!
Angela Then what were you doing in there?
Henry Putting on my aftershave.
Angela Isn't it a bit late to be shaving?
Henry I wasn't shaving!
Angela Then why were you putting on your aftershave?
Henry I'm ... meeting somebody.
Angela (*severely*) You should have vacated this room by midday!
Henry (*puzzled*) Sorry?
Angela You *are* just moving out?
Henry No...!
Angela Yes! *You're* moving out, and I'm moving in.
Henry No!
Angela This *is* the honeymoon suite?
Henry Yes.
Angela And that's a four-poster?
Henry Yes.
Angela Well, the honeymoon suite with a four-poster is where *I* shall be sleeping! (*She puts down her weekend bag on the bed, decisively*)
Henry But this is *our* room!
Angela *Our* room?
Henry *My* room! You'll have to go elsewhere.
Angela (*glaring at him*) There is no "elsewhere"! "Elsewhere" is full! (*She prepares to open her weekend bag*)

In the reception area, Ferris comes out of the kitchen with a tray on which is a bottle of champagne and two glasses. As Henry and Angela are speaking, he crosses briskly and goes out up the R stairs

Henry What about Ferris?
Angela I'm not sharing with him!
Henry He could vacate *his* room and you could move in there.
Angela I have no intention of sleeping between Mr Ferris's sheets. *This* is my room!
Henry (*pathetically*) But I'm already in it…

Ferris comes in

Ferris Here we are! Champagne for the newly-weds!

Henry and Angela look at him in surprise

Angela "Newly-weds"?!
Henry *I* didn't order champagne!
Ferris Then it's a nice surprise, isn't it? (*He sets the tray down on the table and starts to open the bottle*) Nothing like a glass of bubbly to break the ice, I always say. (*Aside to Henry*) You're a bit of a dark horse, aren't you?
Henry Sorry?
Ferris Well… (*He nods, approvingly, at Angela*) …*very* nice…!

The cork comes out

Whoops!
Angela Mr Ferris—we do not want champagne!
Ferris Of course you do. No need to be shy. I expect you're nervous. Never mind. A drop of champers will soon get you going. (*He starts to pour*)
Henry I think there's been a mistake——
Ferris No mistake, sir. (*Rapturously*) The honeymoon suite, a four-poster and a bottle of bubbly. What else could you wish for? The rest is up to you. (*He takes a sip from one of the glasses*) H'm. Very nice. There we are, miss. (*He hands the glass to Angela*)

Angela looks at the glass without enthusiasm

And for you, sir. (*He takes a sip from the other glass and hands it to Henry*)
Angela Mr Ferris! Nobody ordered champagne!
Ferris Don't you worry, miss. It's on the house. My sister's safely out of the way in Benidorm. She'll never find out. Shall I unpack your bag, miss? Lay out your night-dress for you? (*He reaches for her weekend bag, lecherously*)

Angela Leave it where it is!
Ferris Leave it where it is. Right. I quite understand. Shall I send the chambermaid up to do it? She can turn down the bed at the same time.
Angela You don't have to send anyone! I can do everything myself!
Ferris (*quietly*) Yes, I'm sure you can…! I'll leave you to get on with it, then. (*He starts to go*)
Angela Ferris!

Ferris returns at once

Ferris You've changed your mind. I knew you would. (*He reaches for her bag again*)
Angela Leave it where it is! This gentleman will need another room.
Ferris *Another* one?
Henry No, I won't!
Angela Yes, you will! (*To Ferris*) Go and find him another room!
Ferris Oh, that won't be necessary. We're very discreet here. You don't have to keep up appearances. (*He laughs*)
Angela (*firmly*) He *won't* be sleeping here!
Henry Yes, I will!
Angela He won't be sleeping with *me*!

Ferris cannot comprehend this arrangement

Ferris You mean he'll only *visit* you in here—and then go and sleep elsewhere? (*Fed up*) Oh, no! No! There's no point in booking the honeymoon suite if you're going to sleep in separate rooms. (*He starts to go again*)
Angela } (*together*) Ferris!
Henry }

Ferris turns back again

Ferris I'll bring you some nuts.
Henry We don't *want* any nuts!

Ferris gives him a disdainful look

Ferris *You* may not, but the young lady will! You'd like some nuts, wouldn't you, miss? Yes, of course you would. All the young ladies like nuts. And I'll fetch the menu at the same time. (*To Henry*) I expect you'll be having room service? You don't want to tire yourself out going up and down stairs, do you, sir?

Ferris winks at Henry and goes, chuckling happily, closing the door behind him

Henry and Angela are left adrift, each holding a glass of champagne. Uncertain how now to proceed, Henry raises his glass, tentatively

Henry Well—er—perhaps we should raise our glasses?

Angela glares at him

Angela You won't raise anything in *my* bedroom! (*She sits defiantly on the end of the bed*)

Henry sinks into the armchair, suitably rebuffed. Lights out in the Pink Room

In the reception area, Judy comes in from the main entrance, rather apprehensively. She is an awkward, unsophisticated middle-aged woman, a stranger to romantic intrigue. She arrives at the desk and notices a dish of chocolates. She picks one up, nervously, and is about to eat it

Ferris arrives and sees her

Ferris Here!

Judy jumps with fright, throwing the chocolate up into the air. Ferris catches it and eats it himself, glaring at her

You were trying to eat my chocolates!
Judy I ... I was hungry.
Ferris That doesn't mean you can go around eating other people's chocolates!
Judy But I've had a long journey.
Ferris (*relenting*) Oh, all right, then. But only *one*, mind! And leave me the soft centres.

Judy squeezes a few of the chocolates. Ferris watches her in horror

You don't have to squeeze them all!
Judy I'm trying to avoid your soft centres. (*She takes a chocolate and starts to eat it*)
Ferris What do you want, anyway? I'm a busy man.

Judy chews on her hard chocolate and speaks unintelligibly as a result

Judy I've just arrived. It was a long journey from——
Ferris It's no good. I can't hear you.
Judy —and I wasn't sure where I was going to——
Ferris (*holding up a hand*) No, no! I can't stand here listening to all this! I've got a hotel to run. Why are you here anyhow? You delivering something?

Judy shakes her head and hastily swallows the rest of her chocolate

Judy I think I'm coming to stay here.
Ferris No, you're not! (*He indicates the sign*) See? We're fully booked. It's our busy time of the year.
Judy It doesn't *seem* very busy.
Ferris Well, it soon will be!

Judy is about to take another chocolate, but Ferris moves the dish out of her reach

(*Importantly*) I've got a V.I.P. arriving here any minute.
Judy (*impressed*) Really? Who is it? A film star?
Ferris (*disparagingly*) A film star? Of course it's not a film star! It's a journalist. He writes a column about good hotels in one of the better Sunday newspapers. So I can't have people like you hanging about here pinching people's chocolates. It'll lower the tone. What do you want, anyway?

Judy glances around nervously

Judy I ... I'm looking for a man.

Ferris looks at her with a doubtful smile

Ferris You're not, are you?
Judy Yes!
Ferris That *is* a surprise. Any particular man or the first one through the front door?
Judy Of *course* a particular man! What do you take me for?
Ferris I'm not sure... What's he like? (*He indicates a tall man*) Tall?
Judy (*uncertainly*) Er...
Ferris (*indicating a shorter man*) Short?
Judy Medium.
Ferris Medium. Fair?
Judy Er...
Ferris *Dark?*

Judy Er … medium.

Ferris Medium medium. Well, let's see what we can do. (*He consults the register*) Name?

Judy Judy.

Ferris Funny name for a man. Even a medium medium one.

Judy No—that's *my* name!

Ferris You don't look like a Judy to me.

Judy Well, that's what they called me when I was born.

Ferris Really? All right, then—what's *his* name?

Judy Whose name?

Ferris (*trying to be patient*) This man you're supposed to be meeting!

Judy Oh. Henry.

Ferris O'Henry?

Judy No. Just Henry.

Ferris Just Henry. Doesn't he have a second name? We haven't got any "Just Henrys" in the register.

Judy He may not be using it…

Ferris May not be using his second name? Well, what's the purpose of his visit? Perhaps that would help us. What are you meeting him *for*?

Judy Oh, I don't think I can tell you that. It's a secret.

Ferris You don't look like a woman with a secret.

Judy (*disappointed*) Don't I? Well, I *am*!

Ferris Oh. Well, I suppose they do come in all shapes and sizes. Anyway, you'll have wasted your time if you haven't got a booking.

Judy But he said *he*'d do the booking.

Ferris "Just Henry" said he'd do the booking?

Judy Yes.

Ferris For *you*?

Judy For us both. Isn't that what usually happens? The man books the room. Isn't that the usual procedure?

Ferris I can't believe what you're trying to tell me. You mean you and "Just Henry" are going to share the same room?

Judy Yes. Well, I think so. He did say he wanted to sleep with me.

Ferris (*with a smile*) He didn't, did he? What did he want to do that for?

Judy Nobody's ever said they wanted to sleep with me before.

Ferris (*quietly*) I'm not surprised!

Judy What?

Ferris I *am* surprised! And he said he'd do the necessary?

Judy Yes. (*Shyly*) He said he'd booked the honeymoon suite.

Ferris (*amused*) The honeymoon…? (*He freezes, realizing his terrible mistake*) Oh, my God…!

Ferris activates himself and races out up the R *stairs*

Left bewildered, Judy takes a few more chocolates and wanders off into the lounge, hoping to find a more helpful member of staff

Lights up in the Pink Room. Henry and Angela are still sitting in bleak silence with their glasses of champagne

Ferris bursts in breathlessly and stares at Henry

Are you "Just Henry"?
Henry Yes.
Ferris Right! (*He goes quickly to Angela, takes her glass from her, drinks the remaining champagne and puts the glass down abruptly*)

Angela is appalled

Angela Mr Ferris!
Ferris Come along! You can't stay here! (*He grabs her hand and pulls her towards the door*)
Angela What *are* you doing?
Ferris You're in the wrong room!
Angela You said it was the right room.
Ferris I was wrong. It's the wrong room.

Ferris drags the astonished Angela out, slamming the door behind them

Henry, surprised by this unexpected turn of events, smiles happily, puts down his glass and goes into the bathroom

Lights out in the Pink Room

In the reception area, Ferris runs down the R stairs, pulling Angela behind him. He sits her down on the sofa abruptly

You stay there!
Angela (*angrily*) I'd prefer to go back to my room!
Ferris Well, you can't! The honeymoon suite is for the other woman.
Angela What other woman?

Ferris looks and sees that the other woman is no longer present

Ferris Oh my God! *Now* where's she gone to? (*He starts to go, at speed*)
Angela Ferris!

Ferris puts on the brakes

I should like some gin.
Ferris Gin?!
Angela While I'm waiting.
Ferris Gin *now*?
Angela This *is* a hotel, isn't it?
Ferris Yes.
Angela So presumably you have a licence to sell drinks?
Ferris Yes! Yes! (*But he makes no move*)
Angela Then I'd like to have a gin-and-tonic.
Ferris You've just had champagne.
Angela You took it away from me! So now I'd like some gin.
Ferris Well, you'll have to wait! I've got to find the other woman!

Ferris races out to look in the lounge

Angela shakes her head in wonder and goes to study the register

Ferris returns, dragging the astonished Judy behind him

Judy Have you found him, then?
Ferris Your "Just Henry"? Yes! He's upstairs waiting for you. (*He grins cheekily*)
Judy (*losing heart*) Oh, dear. I think I've changed my mind... (*She tries to escape*)

Ferris hangs on to her

Ferris It's too late now to change your mind! Up there to the left! Number Four. You can't miss it. (*He gives her a hefty push*)

Driven by the momentum of the push, Judy goes flying out up the R stairs with her weekend bag

Angela (*astonished*) You're not putting *her* in the honeymoon suite, are you?
Ferris Yes.
Angela Is he expecting her?
Ferris Well, he's going to have a nasty surprise if he's not.
Angela (*jabbing her finger at the register*) See!
Ferris (*jumping*) What?
Angela There I am!
Ferris Where? (*He looks about*)
Angela In the register! There!

Ferris looks at the register, unconvinced

Ferris That's not you, is it?

Angela Yes! It *is*!

Ferris (*after glancing again*) Angela Forward?

Angela Yes!

Ferris But how do I know that that's *you*?

Angela Because I've got a letter from your sister confirming my booking!
I'm in room number twelve. (*She points in the register*) See?

Ferris looks and sees, and is satisfied

Ferris Oh, well, that's all right, then, isn't it? As long as you're legitimate.
(*He laughs*)

Angela (*trying to be patient*) So now perhaps you'd show me to my room?

Ferris I'll go and see if it's ready.

Angela It's bound to be ready! It's after six o'clock!

Ferris All the same, I've got to check, haven't I? The maid may have
forgotten to see to the soap. You stay here! (*He starts to go*)

Angela Then I'll have my gin-and-tonic while I'm waiting.

Ferris Are you a bit of an alcoholic on the quiet?

Angela I will be if I stay here much longer! No, I am not an alcoholic. I would
just like to have an aperitif while I'm waiting for you to show me to my
room.

Ferris Oh, all right. If you say so…

Angela I *do* say so!

*Ferris goes to the drinks trolley, pours a small gin into a very small glass and
brings it to her with a bottle of tonic water. Angela takes it, noticing the size
of the glass*

That's a very small glass.

Ferris I suppose *you* prefer to drink out of a bucket?

Angela gives him a severe look and pours the tonic. Ferris starts to go again

Angela Slice of lemon?

Ferris (*stopping*) What?

Angela I should like a slice of lemon with my gin-and-tonic. If that's not too
much to ask.

*Ferris races to the drinks trolley, returns with a slice of lemon and drops it
into her glass, unceremoniously, causing the gin to splash in her face*

Ferris All right *now*?

Angela (*coldly*) Thank you.
Ferris Right, then. I'll go and check on your room. Make yourself comfortable in the lounge while I'm away. I shan't be long.
Angela I'll try to bear it.

Ferris goes off up the L stairs and Angela goes into the lounge with her gin-and-tonic

Lights up in the Pink Room

The door opens and Judy comes in, still recovering from the momentum of Ferris's push

Henry comes out of the bathroom. He sees Judy and smiles with relief

Henry Judy! You've arrived!
Judy Yes. I *think* so...
Henry I thought you'd never get here.
Judy The taxi driver hadn't even heard of this place.
Henry I'd almost given you up.
Judy (*alarmed*) Given me up? Why should you give me up?
Henry I thought you might have changed your mind.
Judy (*smiling, confidently*) No—I haven't! (*Then she loses confidence*) Yes—I have! (*She makes a dart back towards the door*)
Henry Don't go!

Judy stops uncertainly

You've only just arrived. (*He smiles happily*) You're here now, that's the main thing. (*He holds out his arms to greet her*)

Judy is unsure of the procedure for a moment, then realizes what is expected, and sets off towards his welcoming arms. But her weekend bag ends up between them. She backs off and puts the bag down, embarrassed by her failure

Judy You chose a very isolated place.
Henry (*man of the world*) When you go away with a married woman you've got to be discreet.

Judy is instantly jealous

Judy Have you been away with a *lot* of married women?

Henry No! No, of course not! I didn't mean that.
Judy I thought I was the first.
Henry You are! (*Romantically*) The first and the last.
Judy Good... (*She smiles, happily*)
Henry Well? What do you think of it?
Judy Sorry?
Henry The four-poster! (*He indicates the bed*)
Judy Oh. (*She looks at the bed uncertainly*) I've never slept in a four-poster before.
Henry Neither have I. But I expect we'll soon get into the swing of it.

Judy turns away with a little smile, rather shy in the face of such racy talk and sees the bottle of champagne

Judy Oh, Henry—you ordered champagne! How romantic! (*She goes to it, delightedly*)
Henry Ah—well—no! Actually...
Judy But you might have waited to open it until I got here.
Henry That was Ferris! *He* opened it!
Judy Ferris?
Henry The deputy manager. His sister's in Benidorm.
Judy (*looking more closely at the glasses*) But *both* these glasses have been used!
Henry That was Ferris, too! He opened the champagne and—as you hadn't arrived—I thought it only polite to ask him to join me.
Judy The deputy manager drank some of our champagne?
Henry Yes...
Judy Did you ask him to try the four-poster, as well?
Henry (*forcing a laugh*) Oh, pigeon—you are funny!

Judy smiles at him playfully

Judy Instead of drinking champagne with the deputy manager while you were waiting for me you could have unpacked your bag! (*She giggles in what she imagines is a coquettish manner and goes across to Angela's weekend bag on the bed*)
Henry Ah—er—no—that's not mine.
Judy Then whose is it?
Henry Ah—well—you see——
Judy You mean you've got a strange bag in your bedroom?
Henry (*uncertainly*) Well, I...
Judy We'd better find out who it belongs to, then, hadn't we?
Henry No—no, you mustn't!

Judy opens the bag and takes out a frilly night-dress. She holds it up suspiciously

Judy And I suppose this belongs to Mr Ferris?
Henry He left it here by mistake.
Judy The night-dress?
Henry The suitcase!
Judy Why should he put another lady's suitcase in your bedroom?
Henry It was a mistake!
Judy You've had another woman in here, haven't you?
Henry No! Of course I haven't!
Judy I can smell perfume!
Henry It's my aftershave.
Judy You've been drinking champagne with another woman! You said I was the first and the last!
Henry No!
Judy What?!
Henry Yes! You *are* the first and the last!
Judy You thought I wasn't going to turn up so you found yourself another woman.
Henry Of course I didn't!
Judy Well, there's lipstick on one of the glasses! Don't tell me that Mr Ferris wears lipstick as well as a night-dress! (*She picks up her bag and starts to go*)
Henry Where are you going?
Judy Home! I should never have listened to you!
Henry But you've only just arrived.
Judy Well, I wish I hadn't! I'd gone all my life until now without ever having had an assignation. You told me I'd like it!
Henry You will! We haven't started yet. You're tired after your journey. You'll be all right in a minute.
Judy No, I won't! I'm going!
Henry Your taxi will have gone by now. And you'll never get another one to come to this place!
Judy Then I'll ask Mr Ferris to find me another room. The minute you said you wanted to sleep with me I should have known you were a sex maniac!

Judy goes, slamming the door behind her

Henry (*flattered by the idea*) I'd never thought of myself as a sex maniac...

Henry goes into the bathroom

Lights out in the Pink Room

Judy runs down the R stairs into the reception area

Judy Mr Ferris! Are you there?

Judy goes out into the kitchen

Lights up in the Blue Room

Ferris comes in to check that all is ready. He is surprised to see an open, half-packed suitcase on the bed. He looks about, alert like a bird

Ferris Mr Johnson... Mr Johnson!

A small, vague man in his 70s comes out of the bathroom in his shirt sleeves

Ferris is surprised

What are *you* doing here?

Mr Johnson considers what he was doing

Johnson I'm coming out of the bathroom.
Ferris You're not supposed to *be* here!
Johnson This *is* room number twelve, isn't it?
Ferris Yes. But you're not supposed to be in it!
Johnson I've been in it for the past three days.
Ferris Yes, but your stay ended this morning.
Johnson (*vaguely*) Did it really?
Ferris You know very well it did! (*He indicates the open suitcase on the bed*) That's why you've been packing your things.
Johnson Ah—yes. I wondered why I was doing that. Yes—I was leaving, wasn't I?
Ferris You were supposed to vacate the room by noon!
Johnson Noon, eh? Oh, dear...
Ferris It's a rule of the hotel.
Johnson (*quite pleased*) Well, I've *broken* the rule, then, haven't I?
Ferris Yes—you have! You should have been halfway home by now and the maid should have prepared this room for the next visitor!
Johnson You mean you've got someone else coming to stay in here?
Ferris Yes, of course!
Johnson I'm very surprised...

Ferris hastens to the suitcase and starts finishing off the packing at high speed. Mr Johnson follows him

What are you doing?
Ferris I'm finishing off your packing!
Johnson No, you mustn't!

There is a small contest between them as Ferris packs and Mr Johnson unpacks, frantically, which Ferris finally brings to an end

Ferris You've got to go! There's a lady sleeping here tonight.
Johnson A lady? Oh… (*He remembers vaguely what that is*)
Ferris Don't even *think* about it!
Johnson That's all I *can* do these days…
Ferris You finish off your packing. I'll be back to collect you in five minutes.

Ferris races out

Johnson (*thoughtfully*) I haven't had a lady in my bedroom for years…

Mr Johnson goes back into the bathroom

Lights out in the Blue Room

Ferris races down the stairs into the reception area as Judy comes out of the kitchen and sees him

Judy Ah! There you are, Mr Ferris!
Ferris What were you doing in the kitchen? You can't be hungry. You've just had one of my chocolates.
Judy You'll have to find me another room.
Ferris Another one? Don't you fancy the four-poster?
Judy I'm not staying in there with *him*!
Ferris Oh, dear. Making unreasonable demands, is he? The quiet ones are always the worst.
Judy So you'll have to find somewhere *else* for me to sleep.
Ferris You *are* new to this, aren't you? (*He puts his arm around her shoulders*) You came here to share the honeymoon suite. So sleep isn't on your agenda.
Judy (*escaping from him*) Well, I've changed my mind!
Ferris Then you'll have to unchange it! We haven't *got* another room. (*He indicates the notice*) See? We're fully booked.
Judy What about *your* room?
Ferris No fear! What would my sister say if she came back from Benidorm and found me in bed with one of the guests?
Judy You won't be *with* me!

Ferris (*quietly*) That *is* a relief!

Judy You'll be sleeping elsewhere.

Ferris Oh, no. I've never fancied elsewhere.

Judy So what am I going to do?

Ferris You should have thought of that before you turned your back on the man in the four-poster.

Angela comes in from the lounge

Angela (*calling out*) Well, Mr Ferris? Have you got it ready for me?

Ferris Perhaps you'd like to re-phrase the question.

Angela My room! Is it ready? (*To Judy*) Sorry to interrupt ... but I'm longing for a hot bath. Well, Mr Ferris? Ready or not?

Ferris Not!

Angela Not?!

Ferris There's a bit of a hitch.

Angela A bit of a hitch?! So you don't have a room for me?

Ferris Yes.

Angela You *do* have a room for me?

Ferris Yes.

Judy Which is more than he has for *me*...

Angela turns to Judy

Angela I thought you were in the honeymoon suite with your gentleman?

Ferris She's gone off the idea.

Angela Off the man or off the room?

Judy Both!

Angela (*to Ferris*) Look. If you *do* have a room for me why can't I go into it?

Ferris Because of the hitch!

Angela (*glaring at him*) Well, what *is* the hitch?

Ferris It's not empty.

Angela (*erupting*) Not empty?!

Ferris Not at the moment. But he'll soon be gone.

Angela Are you telling me that there's a man in my bedroom?

Judy There is in *mine*, too!

Ferris Yes.

Angela An unwanted man in my bedroom?

Judy There is in *mine*, too!

Ferris Yes.

Angela I hope you haven't forgotten the rules, Mr Ferris. All rooms have to be vacated by noon on the day of departure.

Ferris That's what I told Mr Johnson! But he hasn't finished packing yet.
Angela I'll give him precisely five minutes.
Ferris Exactly *my* words.
Angela And if he hasn't vacated by then he can finish his packing in the garden!
Ferris What a good idea! (*To Judy*) I hadn't thought of that, had you? Might be rather fun. Packing in the garden. (*He sees her face*) No. Never mind.
Angela And there's something else.
Ferris I thought there might be.
Angela More gin!
Ferris What a surprise!
Angela (*to Judy*) Perhaps you'd care to join me while Mr Ferris tries to find a room for *you* as well?
Judy (*uncertainly*) Well, I——
Ferris Oh, go on, dear! You join her for gin. (*He pushes her across to Angela*)
Angela Two large G-and-Ts in the lounge, Mr Ferris. (*To Judy*) After you.
Judy Oh—right.

Judy goes into the lounge

Ferris starts to go towards the stairs

Angela Gin *now*, Mr Ferris!
Ferris Gin now. Right.

Angela follows Judy into the lounge

Ferris trots across to the drinks trolley to sort out the gin-and-tonics

Henry comes down the R stairs

Ferris, busy, sees him

Didn't take *you* long to put the cat among the pigeons, did it?
Henry It's all your fault!
Ferris Yes, I thought it would be.
Henry You sent up the wrong woman!
Ferris Took you a long time to find out.
Henry Where is she?
Ferris Which one?
Henry The second one, of course!
Ferris Oh, she's in the lounge with the *other* one.
Henry (*alarmed*) You mean they're in there *together*?

Ferris Yes. Both gasping for gin.

Angela looks in from the lounge

Angela (*bellowing*) Ferris! Gin!
Ferris (*to Henry*) See what I mean? (*Going to Angela*) Just coming, madam!
Angela (*impatiently*) Oh, give it to *me*!

Angela takes the tray of drinks from Ferris and goes back into the lounge

Ferris goes to Henry, urgently

Ferris You'll have to go and make it up with your funny friend. (*He tries to urge him on his way*)
Henry (*resisting*) I don't think she wants me to...
Ferris Then you'll have to persuade her, won't you? I don't expect she'll take much persuading. The hotel's fully booked—and now I've got this journalist bloke arriving!
Henry The one you thought was me?
Ferris Yes! He writes a critical column about hotels in a Sunday newspaper, so I've got to make a good impression, haven't I?
Henry But why don't you know his name?
Ferris Because my sister rang off without telling me and I haven't got her number!
Henry So how do you know that it's a man?

Ferris looks at him blankly for a second

Ferris What?
Henry Well ... it could be a woman, couldn't it?
Ferris (*thinking hard*) Yes. Yes, I suppose it could. I hadn't thought of that. How the hell am I going to find out?
Henry (*laughing*) You'll just have to wait and see what turns up, won't you?
Ferris You go and make peace with your friend while I get Mr Johnson out of number twelve! (*He starts to go*)
Henry Ferris!
Ferris (*stopping*) What?
Henry (*puzzled*) Why am I doing this?

Ferris returns to him

Ferris Because you want to *help* me.
Henry Oh. I didn't know that... (*He thinks about it*)

Ferris And I'm very grateful. Thank you, sir.

Henry Thank *you*, Ferris. (*He holds out his hand*)

Reluctantly, Ferris passes some money back to Henry, who grins triumphantly

Ferris (*going*) I wish *I* was the one lying on a beach in Benidorm…

Ferris goes out up the L stairs

Angela comes in from the lounge

Henry looks at her in surprise

Henry You haven't finished that gin already?

Angela It was only a very small one. (*She goes to him with a smile*) You *are* in trouble, aren't you?

Henry (*nervously*) Am I?

Angela You'd better speak to your lady friend. She thinks you've got another woman on the go!

Henry (*gloomily*) Yes, I know… She saw the champagne and put two and two together. *You* know what women are like! Yes, of course you do…

Angela Where's Mr Ferris?

Henry He's seeing to your room.

Angela And about time, too! When he comes back tell him I'm upstairs—and waiting! (*She starts to go, then hesitates*) I can tell you one thing—I'm not very impressed by the way this hotel is run. I shall have to make a note of it. (*She continues on her way out*)

Henry jumps to the obvious conclusion

Henry Oh, no…! Just a minute!

Angela (*stopping again*) Yes?

Henry (*in awe*) It's *you*, isn't it?

Angela What's me?

Henry You mustn't say nasty things about Ferris. I'm sure he's doing his best.

Angela (*severely*) Well, his best isn't good enough, is it?

Angela goes out up the R stairs

Music plays as Henry goes into the lounge to find Judy

Lights up in the Pink Room

Angela comes in, sees her night-dress on the bed and is puzzled

She puts it into her weekend bag and fastens it. Then she notices the champagne. The temptation being too great, she pours herself a generous glass and sits down to wait for Ferris

Lights out in the Pink Room. Lights up in the Blue Room

Ferris comes in, looking about. No sign of Mr Johnson

The music stops

Ferris Mr Johnson! (*He closes the suitcase and fastens it*) Mr Johnson!

Mr Johnson comes out of the bathroom, a little unsteadily

Ferris claps his hands impatiently

Come on! Chop-chop! Time's up!
Johnson (*feebly*) I may have to stay in my room a little longer...
Ferris You can't! This room isn't your room any more. It's somebody else's room now.
Johnson The lady you told me about?
Ferris Yes. And she'll be up here any minute!
Johnson Perhaps I could stay here another night?
Ferris I doubt if she'd agree.
Johnson I could go first thing in the morning.
Ferris No! Time's up! You go now.
Johnson But I'm not feeling very well... (*He goes towards the bed, hoping for rest*)

Ferris intercepts him and keeps him on his feet

Ferris That's not my fault! What have you been eating?
Johnson I only had lunch.
Ferris I hope you're not casting aspersions on our chef?
Johnson Oh, no!
Ferris I should hope not. Our chef's reputation is second to none. (*He peers at him suspiciously*) Did you bring something in with you? Stale sandwich? Something like that?
Johnson No!
Ferris A likely tale! I expect your pocket's full of crumbs. (*He tries to look*)
Johnson Perhaps if I have a little rest... (*He starts to sit on the bed again*)

Ferris intercepts him once more and keeps him on his feet

Ferris No, you won't! Come along! Off we go! (*He half carries the old man towards the door*)
Johnson But my suitcase…!
Ferris I'll come back for that. I can't carry you *and* a suitcase!

Ferris and Mr Johnson go, closing the door behind them

Lights out in the Blue Room

In the reception area, Henry and Judy come out of the lounge, their arms around each other, the picture of contentment

Judy I should never have doubted you.
Henry Of course you shouldn't, you foolish pigeon.
Judy I just put two and two together.
Henry You never were good at sums.

They start to go towards the R *stairs as Ferris arrives with an old man under his arm*

Ferris (*to Henry, breathlessly*) Come and give me a hand!
Henry (*seeing them*) Oh, my God! (*To Judy*) You go ahead, pigeon. I shan't be long. (*He kisses her briefly*)

Judy is embarrassed by being kissed in public, giggles and runs out up the R *stairs*

Henry goes to Ferris

What have you got there?
Ferris It's Mr Johnson.
Henry What?
Ferris Mr Johnson out of number twelve!
Henry (*peering at him*) Is he all right?
Ferris Of course he's all right. That's what he looks like.
Henry Is he leaving, then?
Ferris He'd better be!
Henry Hasn't he got a suitcase with him?
Ferris Yes. But we can't put him in that.

Henry has another look at Mr Johnson

Henry (*whispering*) Do you think he can hear what we're saying?

Johnson Yes. You're going to put me in a suitcase.

Ferris Of course we're not going to put you in a suitcase! It wouldn't be big enough.

Henry What *are* you going to do with him?

Ferris I'll call him a taxi.

Henry You don't know where he's going.

Ferris He's got a tongue in his head, hasn't he?

Johnson I'd rather go back to my room...

Ferris You haven't got a room!

Johnson I don't feel very well...

Henry What's the matter with him?

Ferris Don't ask me. *I*'m not a doctor. I think he's eaten a stale sandwich. He'll be as right as rain in no time.

Johnson But I never ate a stale sandwich...

Ferris Well, that's what they all say, isn't it? (*To Henry*) We'll put him in the lounge until his taxi gets here.

Henry In the lounge? He'll be in the walking way.

Ferris What?

Henry People might trip over him.

Ferris *He* won't mind!

Henry and Ferris pick up Mr Johnson and carry him into the lounge

Lights up in the Pink Room. Angela is sitting patiently, sipping champagne

Judy comes in, still smiling after her kiss, sees Angela and stops smiling

Judy What are *you* doing in here?

Angela Fetching my suitcase.

Judy So it was *yours*?

Angela Yes.

Judy What was your suitcase doing in my bedroom?

Angela Your bedroom? I thought you'd gone off the idea.

Judy Well, now I'm back on it again!

Angela It was a mistake.

Judy It certainly was!

Angela *Ferris*'s mistake!

Judy You're sitting down! If you only came to fetch your suitcase, why are you sitting down?

Angela I'm waiting for Ferris to get my room ready.

Judy You're drinking my champagne!

Angela It's not yours. It's mine. He gave it to me.

Judy He brought the champagne for *you*?!

Angela For both of us!

Judy (*dramatically*) Henry bought you champagne! No wonder you offered me gin. You were waiting here for Henry!

Angela No, no! For Ferris! He's seeing to my room. There's a man in it. Remember?

Judy *Another* one? I don't believe you!

Angela Ask your gentleman friend, then.

Judy What's the point? He never seems to tell me the truth. I knew I should never have succumbed to the temptations of lust.

Judy goes in an aura of disenchantment

Angela looks surprised, picks up her case and goes out, closing the door behind her

Lights out in the Pink Room

In the reception area, Henry comes in from the lounge as Judy runs down the R *stairs in a fury. She stops, facing him*

I'm not speaking to you!

Henry (*surprised*) You were a moment ago. What's the matter, pigeon?

Judy You know very well what's the matter! One minute you try to seduce me and the next you cast me aside! Aaaagh!

Judy runs out into the kitchen, crying noisily

Henry is left bewildered by this sudden about-face

Angela arrives down the R *stairs*

Henry She's crying again. What have you been telling her?

Angela She keeps misunderstanding things. Where's Ferris?

Henry In there with Mr Johnson.

Angela Ah! So my room must be ready, then.

Henry Oh, yes—yes, I'm sure it will be!

Angela About time, too! I'm surprised this hotel has got any stars at all.

Angela goes up the L *stairs with her suitcase*

Ferris returns from the lounge

Henry goes to him urgently

Henry Ah—Ferris! I've got good news!

Ferris smiles delightedly

Ferris You've made it up with your lady friend!
Henry No, no!
Ferris You *haven't* made it up with your lady friend?
Henry Well, I had. But now I haven't.
Ferris Had but haven't? I can't keep up with your sex life. (*He goes towards the desk*)
Henry Ferris! I was right. It *is* a woman!
Ferris Well, of course it is! Otherwise, you wouldn't have brought her with you, would you? (*Then doubtfully*) It *is* a woman, isn't it?
Henry Not Judy! The one your sister telephoned from Benidorm about!
Ferris The Sunday newspaper person?
Henry Yes! It *is* a woman!
Ferris How do *you* know?
Henry Because she's arrived. She's here!
Ferris And she's a woman?
Henry No doubt about it. And what's more—you've already seen her!
Ferris When?
Henry When you sent her up to me in the honeymoon suite!
Ferris (*appalled*) Miss Forward? Oh, no! But how do you know that it's her?
Henry Because she said she was making notes about the hotel!

Ferris freezes for a moment, then hops about with anxiety as he recalls his many lapses

Ferris And I didn't even have her room ready! And I refused to give her a gin! And I asked if she preferred to drink out of a bucket! It'll be all over the newspapers!
Henry You'll have to make up for lost time, then, won't you?
Ferris Yes. Yes, I will. I'll do it now. (*A beat*) How?
Henry *I* don't know! (*Encouragingly*) But you're the deputy manager. You'll think of something.
Ferris Where is she now?
Henry Gone to her room.

Ferris clutches Henry in a panic and shakes him

Ferris But it hasn't even been serviced! And there's an old man's suitcase on the bed! I knew I shouldn't have let my sister go to Benidorm. (*He casts Henry aside, and then thinks of something*) Ah! Wait a minute!

Henry You've thought of something.
Ferris Yes.
Henry I knew you would.
Ferris *You*'ll have to help me.
Henry (*nervously*) Me? No!
Ferris You—yes! This newspaper person...
Henry What about her?
Ferris She ought to have the best room, wouldn't you say?
Henry (*considering*) Well, yes, Ferris. I would have thought so. If you want to make a good impression.
Ferris And which room would you say that is?
Henry Well. *I* don't know, do I?
Ferris Yes, you do.
Henry Do I?
Ferris (*impressively*) The honeymoon suite!
Henry But *I*'m in there!
Ferris Yes. You were. But now you're not. *She*'s going to have it.
Henry Is she?
Ferris Well, you did say she should have the best room.
Henry Did I?
Ferris Just now.
Henry Oh. But where will *I* be?
Ferris You'll be in Mr Johnson's room.

Henry clutches Ferris in a panic, and shakes him, as Ferris did him a moment ago

Henry But it hasn't even been serviced yet! And there's an old man's suitcase on the bed!

Ferris escapes from Henry's clutches

Ferris Pull yourself together! It'll soon be ready. Then you can go into his room.
Henry (*sulking a litle*) No, Ferris. That's not fair. I booked the honeymoon suite.
Ferris Well, it's not much use to you if your funny friend keeps crying all the time.
Henry No! I won't do it!
Ferris You said you were going to help me.
Henry No. *You* said I was going to help you.
Ferris But this is an emergency! Surely you'll help in an emergency? You don't look like the sort of man who wouldn't help in an emergency.

Henry (*flattered*) Don't I?
Ferris No.
Henry Oh…
Ferris So you'll do it, then?
Henry (*relenting*) Well, I suppose I would like to help in an emergency…
Ferris (*with a big smile*) Thank you, sir!
Henry Thank *you*, Ferris. (*He holds out his hand, pointedly*)

Reluctantly, Ferris returns his second tip to Henry, who smiles triumphantly

Ferris That's settled, then. *You* go and get your things out of the honeymoon suite, and *I'll* go and find the lady.

Ferris and Henry race out up opposite stairs

As they disappear, Edgar comes in from the main entrance, looking about, unfamiliar with the surroundings. He is a rather pompous man in his 60s, carrying a small suitcase

Judy returns from the kitchen

They see each other and are surprised

Judy Edgar!
Edgar Judy!

Pause

     Judy!
Judy Edgar!
Edgar Well, at least we know who we are. Aren't you going to embrace me?
Judy What?
Edgar I am your husband. You usually embrace me.
Judy Yes. Of course.

They embrace perfunctorily

     (*Aside*) What's he doing here?
Edgar (*aside*) This *is* a surprise!

They come out of their embrace

Judy What are you doing here?

Edgar This *is* a surprise! I didn't expect to see *you* here.

Judy I... I'm here for a break.

Edgar From me?

Judy You said you were going away.

Edgar I *am* away. I'm here. That's away, isn't it? But what are *you* doing here? You don't usually go away and stay in hotels all on your own.

Judy No! I don't, do I?

Edgar It's out of character.

Judy Yes! It is! I can't think what came over me.

Edgar So why did you do it?

Judy I... I wanted to try something different.

Edgar (*generously*) And why not? I expect you were bored with what you were getting at home.

Judy Yes, Edgar. Just a little...

Edgar I can understand. Same old food. Day after day. You needed a change.

Judy Yes...

Edgar Nothing like hotel food to give you a lift. So *that's* why you came here? To try something different. Toad-in-the-hole?

Judy Very possibly. I just wanted to do something I've never done before.

Edgar You should have consulted *me*! I could have given you advice.

Judy (*quietly*) No, you couldn't...!

Edgar I stay in a lot of hotels.

Judy (*aside*) I can't think what he's doing here. (*To Edgar*) What are you doing here?

Edgar Business. I'm on business.

Judy What a coincidence!

Edgar *You're* not on business.

Judy You and me being here in the same hotel!

Edgar Ah—yes. (*Noticing*) You've been crying!

Judy Have I?

Edgar Your eyes are red. Have you been shedding tears?

Judy Well ... just a few.

Edgar A few too many! Has somebody been making you cry? If somebody's been making you cry I shall kill him!

Judy You don't have to do that! I... I was lonely. I often cry when I'm lonely.

Edgar Well, you won't be lonely now that *I'm* here.

Judy No...

Edgar Darling! (*He holds out his arms, dramatically*)

Dutifully, she goes into his arms and they embrace. Over her shoulder we see an anxious man. They come out of their embrace

Judy We'll have to find Ferris.

Edgar Ferris?

Judy He's the manager.

Edgar Is he missing?

Judy No, no! He's standing in for his sister. She's in Benidorm.

Edgar What the hell's she doing in Benidorm?

Judy Escaping, I imagine.

Edgar Is somebody pursuing her?

Judy From the weather! She's escaping from the weather. So we'll find
  Ferris. He'll know where you'll be sleeping.

Edgar Well ... presumably *you* have a room?

Judy It's—it's very small! Like a box room. Hardly space for one!

Edgar Space is of no account to married people.

Judy Isn't it? Mr Ferris wasn't in the kitchen, so he's probably through here.
  I'll show you the way.

Nervously, Judy leads the way into the lounge

Edgar follows her, thoughtfully

Edgar (*aside*) I wonder what she's *doing* here...

Edgar goes into the lounge

Lights up in the Blue Room

A knock at the door, then Ferris comes in nervously

Ferris Miss Forward?

Angela comes out of the bathroom with her weekend bag

Angela There's no soap in the bathroom.

*Ferris assumes an air of extreme civility, bowing from time to time with
overdone politeness*

Ferris Miss Forward—you should have allowed me to carry your case. We
  don't allow guests to carry their cases. Not in *this* hotel. (*He reaches for
  her case*)

She wrestles it back from him

Angela It's a very small case. I'm quite capable of carrying it myself.

Ferris But your comfort is our chief concern... (*He bows low*)

Angela puts down her case and looks at him, surprised by his change of attitude

Angela What's the matter with you, Ferris? You weren't so polite when I was asking for gin.
Ferris (*full of regret*) Ah, no—and I do apologise.
Angela (*surprised*) You *do*?
Ferris Oh, yes. I was under pressure at the time. I'm not used to the stresses and strains of hotel management. I beg your indulgence for any small hiccup that may have occurred during my sister's temporary absence in Benidorm.

Angela looks at him with extreme suspicion

Angela Ferris—what are you up to?
Ferris Up to, miss? (*He laughs*) Ah—you will have your little joke!
Angela It wasn't a joke.
Ferris (*quietly*) What a pity...! I'm afraid there's been a dreadful mistake. And it was all my fault.
Angela It certainly was! That funny woman's been crying ever since.
Ferris Sorry? (*He realizes what she means*) Ah—no—not that!
Angela You mean you've made more than one mistake? You have something *else* to apologise for?

Ferris manages to control his natural manner and sustains his civility

Ferris Let me take your case, miss. (*He reaches for her case*)

Again she retrieves it

Angela Ferris! Will you stop trying to pick up my suitcase!
Ferris But you shouldn't *be* here, miss! You should be elsewhere.
Angela But I've only just got here!
Ferris You shouldn't be in *this* room!
Angela I hope you're not expecting me to vacate this room when I've only just moved in?
Ferris Not exactly, but——
Angela Then perhaps you'd kindly remove Mr Johnson's suitcase from my bed?
Ferris But I don't have to remove it.
Angela You're not suggesting that I share a room with Mr Johnson?

Ferris Oh, no! You see, this isn't your room any longer.

Angela It was a moment ago.

Ferris That was a mistake! My sister and I want you to have the *best* room.

Angela Why?

Ferris (*fawning, suitably*) Your comfort is our chief concern…

Angela You said that before.

Ferris So I'm moving you… (*with great effect*) ..into the honeymoon suite!

Angela But you've only just moved me *out* of the honeymoon suite!

Ferris Ah—yes. That was a mistake.

Angela *Another* one? Are you trying to get into the Guinness Book of Records?

Ferris You see, I didn't know *then* what I know *now*.

Angela Do you always talk in riddles, Mr Ferris? What didn't you know?

Ferris I didn't know then that you were a woman.

Angela How very disappointing.

Ferris You see, I was expecting a man.

Angela Do you know *many* men called Angela Forward?

Ferris (*with a nervous laugh*) I didn't know then that it was *you*. But now that I know that it's you it makes all the difference.

Angela I'm surprised you *noticed* the difference.

Ferris And that's why I'm moving you back into the honeymoon suite.

Angela Why?

Ferris Because it's the best room in the hotel. And that's the room we want you to have. (*He makes another dive at her suitcase*)

Angela You're doing it again! (*She retrieves it once more*) Mr Ferris, I cannot move into the honeymoon suite!

Ferris Why not?

Angela Because there's a man already in there with a crying woman. Or had you forgotten?

Ferris Oh, they won't be in there! They'll be in *this* room and you'll be in *their* room.

Angela Why?

Ferris Why do you keep saying "why"?

Angela I've got an enquiring mind. Why should I want the honeymoon suite when I'm here on my own?

Ferris tries to think of a reason

Ferris You like to stretch? (*He demonstrates stretching*)

Angela Stretch?!

Ferris It's a very big bed. Ideal for stretching. (*He demonstrates again*)

Angela I don't want to stretch!

Ferris (*desperately*) Please do as I say, Miss Forward! My sister would expect me to make sure that you're made comfortable and given everything that you want.

Angela relents wearily

Angela Oh ... very well, then. If you insist.
Ferris (*smiling, sycophantically*) We aim to give satisfaction. (*He bows humbly*)
Angela You're giving me the honeymoon suite. That's quite enough to be going on with.
Ferris I'll take your case. (*He dives at her case again*)
Angela No!! (*She clutches it, protectively*)

Ferris indicates the door politely

Ferris After you, Miss Forward.
Angela No fear! After *you*!

Angela pushes Ferris out ahead of her

Lights out in the Blue Room

In the reception area, Henry is coming down the R stairs with his overnight bag. Judy is coming out of the lounge. They meet

Judy Something awful's happened!
Henry Yes. *You*'re not speaking to me.
Judy (*noticing his bag*) Ah! You're leaving. That is a relief.
Henry I'm not leaving!
Judy It might be advisable.
Henry To leave?
Judy Yes.
Henry Why?
Judy It would help to solve my problem.
Henry Which problem is that?
Judy My husband's arrived!
Henry Arrived where?
Judy *Here!* He's in the lounge.
Henry You never told me your husband was coming as well!
Judy I didn't know! He said he was going away on business.
Henry You didn't tell him you were coming here?
Judy Of course not! But you know what jealous husbands are like.
Henry *Is* he jealous?
Judy He will be if he finds out.

Henry Violently jealous?
Judy I wouldn't be surprised.
Henry You didn't tell him about *me*, did you?
Judy Henry! You should be worrying about *me*!

Ferris comes down the L stairs, followed by Angela, who is carrying her weekend bag

Judy sees Ferris

Mr Ferris! I must speak to you!

Ferris gives her a disdainful look

Ferris You can't speak to me *now*! I'm taking this lady up to the honeymoon suite. (*He turns to Angela with a sycophantic smile*) You follow close behind me, Miss Forward.
Angela (*wearily*) Ferris, I think I *can* find my own way. I have been in there before, remember.
Judy Yes, she certainly has! (*She starts to cry again*)
Angela (*to Ferris*) You see what I mean?

Angela goes out up the R stairs

Judy glares at Henry

Judy It didn't take *you* long to find a replacement!
Henry Look—I can explain!
Ferris Don't you worry, miss. Everything's all right. I've got another room for you two.
Judy I'm not sleeping with *him*!

Ferris turns to Henry, at a loss to understand

Ferris I thought that was what you came here to do?
Henry Yes, but I can't do it anymore.
Ferris Why? What have you done to yourself?
Henry She's married!
Ferris You *knew* she was married!
Henry But he's here!
Ferris Who?
Henry Her husband!
Ferris *Here?*
Henry Yes!

Ferris *Here* here? *In—this—hotel* here?
Henry Yes!
Ferris (*an appalling thought*) Not Mr Johnson?
Henry ⎫ (*together*) No!
Judy ⎭
Ferris You mean somebody *else* has arrived?
Henry Yes.
Ferris When I was upstairs seeing to the other lady?
Henry ⎫ (*together*) Yes!
Judy ⎭
Ferris Well. I hope he's got a booking.
Henry He doesn't need one.
Ferris Of course he needs one! We can't have people sleeping on the floor.
Henry Ferris—he'll be sleeping with his wife!
Ferris Will he? (*To Judy*) Will he?
Judy (*not keen*) Well, I suppose so. He is my husband.

Ferris turns to Henry

Ferris You're not thinking of making it a threesome, are you?
Henry No fear!

Edgar marches in from the lounge and sees Ferris

Edgar Ah! You must be the missing manager.
Ferris Missing?

Henry looks puzzled

Henry You're not missing, are you, Ferris?
Ferris I wish I was! (*To Edgar*) No, I'm not missing.
Henry He's not the manager either.
Ferris No. I'm standing in for my sister. She's in Benidorm.
Edgar Ah—yes! The one who's escaping.

Ferris and Henry exchange a look

Ferris ⎫ (*together*) Escaping?!
Henry ⎭
Edgar (*to Judy*) You *said* she was escaping.
Judy Only from the weather! (*She looks helplessly at Henry*)
Ferris So *she's* not escaping and *I'm* not missing.
Edgar You were when I arrived.
Ferris Was I? I don't remember being missing…

Edgar You were missing from your post!
Ferris Which post is that?
Edgar The position you should have been in.
Ferris I'm not sure what position that is. (*He looks at Henry for assistance*)
Edgar Here! At reception! To welcome the new arrivals.
Ferris Oh, them! I didn't think there were going to be any more of them.
Henry (*aside to Ferris*) No, there shouldn't have been...!
Edgar You should have been present—and erect!
Ferris Oh, I'm never that!

Edgar is looking at Judy, puzzled

Edgar Have you been crying again?
Ferris No. I haven't cried since Christmas.
Edgar Not you! *Her!* (*To Judy*) Have you?
Judy No!
Edgar You *look* as if you've been crying.
Henry You probably gave her a surprise. Arriving unexpectedly like that. Enough to make *anyone* cry.
Ferris Why aren't *you* crying, then? (*He laughs*)

Henry glares at Ferris

Judy This is my husband—Edgar.
Ferris Yes, I thought it might be...!
Henry (*to Edgar*) So she probably cried when she saw *you*.

Edgar glares at him

With joy! At seeing you!
Edgar How do *you* know what makes my wife cry?
Henry Er... Ferris told me.
Edgar What the hell does *he* know about it?
Henry He's standing in for his sister.
Ferris Yes. And people who stand in for their sisters have to know everything.
Edgar Do you have *many* guests bursting into tears?
Ferris Only when other people's husbands turn up...

Henry glares at Ferris. Edgar goes to Judy, puzzled

Edgar Why should you be crying? You can't be lonely now *I'm* here. (*To the others*) She always cries when she's lonely.

Ferris So do I! Sometimes, all alone in the middla of the night, I'm quite uncontrollable.

Edgar goes to peer at Henry, suspiciously

Edgar Just a minute! Who *are* you?
Henry (*nervously*) I—I—I'm a guest! And I'm just on my way to my room. (*He tries to escape*)
Edgar Just a minute!

Henry puts on the brakes

What are you doing here?
Ferris Well, he won't be doing what he was *going* to be doing…!

Henry gives Ferris a look, then turns back to Edgar

Henry I'm here on business.
Ferris (*quietly*) And his business is nobody's business.
Edgar (*suspiciously*) I hope you haven't been making my wife cry.
Henry I didn't know she *was* your wife…!
Edgar What?!
Henry No! I've never seen her before!
Edgar Have you just arrived, then?
Henry Oh, yes! This very minute!
Edgar So that's why you're carrying your bag?

Henry glances down and sees that this is true

Henry Good Lord, so I am.
Edgar (*turning to Ferris*) *You* should be carrying his bag.
Ferris I've got a bad back.
Judy (*sweetly*) No, Edgar. The porter carries bags.
Edgar (*to Ferris*) Have you *got* a porter?
Ferris I'm not sure. (*To Henry*) Have I?
Henry No.
Ferris (*to Edgar*) No.
Edgar Then *you* should be carrying bags, bad back or no bad back.
Ferris I have been trying.
Edgar (*indicating Henry*) With him?
Ferris No. With one of the ladies. I tried with her but I was spurned.
Edgar (*quietly*) I'm not surprised…!
Henry Dont't worry. He can carry *your* bag.

Edgar I never trust people to carry my bag. (*He turns abruptly to Judy*) Come along, then! Which room are we in?

Judy It's a very small room! Far too small for two!

Henry Yes. Haven't you got a room of your own?

Edgar No point in having two rooms.

Ferris (*aside*) Oh, yes, there is...!

Edgar It'll soon be time for dinner, so let's go to your room and freshen up.

Judy hesitates, not knowing which room she is in

Come along! Lead the way!

Judy Er... (*She goes to Ferris, confidentially*) Which room is it, Mr Ferris?

Edgar (*laughing*) Don't say you can't remember the number of your own room!

Judy Well. I haven't been in it very long... (*She looks back at Ferris*)

Ferris (*whispering behind his hand*) Number Twelve.

Judy Oh, yes! (*To Edgar*) Number Twelve! (*She starts to go, then stops and returns to Ferris*) I've forgotten which way that is.

Edgar Forgotten?!

Ferris points her in the direction of the L stairs and gives her a gentle push

Judy (*going*) Yes! Now I remember!

Edgar gives the others a look and follows Judy off up the L stairs

Ferris Poor little woman. Fancy being married to him. No wonder she came here with you.

Henry (*smiling, gratefully*) Oh, thank you, Ferris. (*Then doubtfully*) That *was* a compliment, wasn't it?

The phone rings. They jump in unison. Ferris answers the phone

Lights up in the Pink Room. Angela is on the phone

Angela Ferris?

Ferris (*hastily resuming sycophancy*) Ah—Miss Forward! What can I do for you?

Angela I'm in the honeymoon suite—and waiting.

Ferris Waiting?

Angela For you!

Ferris Waiting for *me*? (*He looks fearfully at Henry*)

Angela You should have been here by now.

Ferris Ah—I didn't realize that...

Angela You *should* have realized!

Ferris Yes—and I do apologise.

Angela Ferris! Do you know what I'm talking about?

Ferris I'm not sure…

Angela Gin!

Ferris I might have guessed…!

Angela It's time for my aperitif.

Ferris *Again?* I'll come straight up.

Angela I shall be waiting. (*She hangs up and goes to the bed to start unpacking her weekend bag*)

Ferris also hangs up

Henry Good Lord, Ferris, you've gone quite pale.

Ferris I'm not surprised. She's calling for gin again. (*He hastens to the drinks trolley*)

Henry Is that all? I thought she was calling for *you!*

Ferris pours a large gin and opens a small bottle of tonic water

(*Deep in thought*) Mind you, from now on I suppose you'll have to give her everything she wants.

Ferris (*alarmed*) Will I?

Henry Well … you don't want her to write nasty things about your sister's hotel, do you?

Ferris No fear! (*He heads for the* R *stairs with the gin-and-tonic*)

Henry I'll say goodbye, then.

Ferris (*hesitating*) Why? Where are you going?

Henry I'm going home, of course! I'm not staying here to be killed by Edgar.

Ferris (*aghast*) You're going to leave me?

Henry You'll get over it, Ferris. After all, we haven't known each other very long.

Ferris Leave me with all this confusion!

Henry Isn't that what hotel management is all about? Learning to cope with confusion?

Henry smiles sagely and goes out to the main entrance with his bag

Ferris I knew I should have gone to Benidorm…

Ferris hastens out up the R *stairs with the gin-and-tonic*

In the Pink Room, Angela is unpacking. She takes out her night-dress and lays it on the bed artistically. A knock at the door

Angela Come in!

Ferris comes in

Ferris Your gin-and-tonic, Miss Forward.
Angela About time, too.
Ferris Sorry if I kept you waiting. I'll put it down here, shall I? (*He sets the gin down on the table*)
Angela Oo, that *is* a large one!
Ferris Sorry?
Angela It's all right. I'm not complaining.

Ferris hesitates

Pour the tonic, Ferris.
Ferris Pour the tonic. Right.

There is only room in the glass for the very smallest drop of tonic, which Ferris pours with aplomb

There we are, miss. To your liking, I hope. Your wish is our command. (*He bows low*)
Angela Well? Have you brought it with you?
Ferris Sorry?
Angela The menu.
Ferris Menu!
Angela For dinner! You do serve dinner?
Ferris Ah—you'll be eating, then?
Angela Of course I'll be eating!
Ferris Of course you will. I'll get the menu right away. (*He starts to go*)
Angela And, Ferris…!

Ferris hesitates

Ferris Yes, miss?
Angela (*with a smile*) Don't be long.
Ferris No. Right.

Ferris scuttles out

Angela sits down and sips her large gin, gratefully. Lights out in the Pink Room. Lights up in the Blue Room

Edgar and Judy come in. He looks about without enthusiasm

Edgar Is *this* your room?
Judy Er—yes. I think so…

Edgar is surprised by her vagueness

Edgar You have seen it before?
Judy Oh, yes! Yes, of course. I *think* so…
Edgar (*aside*) She was right. It is a bit small. (*To Judy*) You were right. It is a bit small.
Judy Yes! I told you! It's far too small for two!

Edgar sees the suitcase on the bed and goes to look at it

Edgar I don't think I've seen this suitcase of yours before. Is it new?
Judy Oh, that isn't mine.
Edgar Not *yours*?
Judy No. It belongs to somebody else.

Edgar is immediately suspicious

Edgar I thought so! So *that's* why you're here! (*He opens the lid of the suitcase abruptly*) Ah! Men's pyjamas! I might have guessed. I should have known that you were a woman of easy virtue. (*He closes the lid*) You've got another man in here, haven't you?
Judy (*horrified*) No! Not *now*.
Edgar Not *now*?!
Judy Not at all!
Edgar Too small for two if it's your husband, but not too small for two if you're not married to each other!
Judy I can explain…!
Edgar When I find him I'll kill him!

Edgar picks up the suitcase and goes angrily

Alarmed, Judy goes into the bathroom as the Lights go out in the Blue Room

In the reception area, Ferris comes down the R stairs as Mr Johnson comes in from the lounge

Ferris You can't come in here!
Johnson But I've been out there rather a long time.
Ferris You had a glass of water! What more do you want?
Johnson I want to go back to my room. (*He starts to go*)

Ferris cuts him off and brings him back again

Ferris You haven't got a room.
Johnson I'm not feeling very well... (*He teeters, precariously*)

Ferris catches him

Ferris You're not going to faint, are you?
Johnson Very probably! (*He starts to faint and clings on to Ferris*)
Ferris I told you to sit down in there until your taxi arrives. You're bound to feel faint if you go galloping about like this!

Edgar comes down the L stairs, carrying Mr Johnson's suitcase

Edgar There's another man's suitcase in my wife's bedroom! When I find who it belongs to, I'll kill him!
Johnson (*seeing it, delightedly*) Ooh—my suitcase...!
Edgar Yours?!
Ferris Well, aren't you going to kill him? It won't be very difficult. He's half dead already.

Angela runs down the R stairs

Angela Ferris! You forgot my slice of lemon! (*She stops, seeing Edgar, and is surprised*)

Edgar sees her, and is appalled

Edgar!
Edgar Angela!
Ferris Don't tell me you two *know* each other?
Angela (*with a big smile*) Yes, we certainly do!
Edgar Oh, my God!

In panic, Edgar starts to go but collides with Ferris who, in turn, collides with Mr Johnson. They collapse on to the sofa, clinging together as——

Edgar races out into the garden with Angela watching in amazement

Black-out

CURTAIN

ACT II

The same. A few minutes later

Angela and Edgar have gone. Ferris and Mr Johnson are still sitting silently together, Ferris's arm around him

Nobody speaks for a moment

Johnson (*quietly*) Whatever's going on?
Ferris *I* don't know...

A pause

Johnson There were two *other* people here a moment ago.
Ferris Yes...

A pause

Johnson Then one of them disappeared into the garden.
Ferris Yes...

A pause

Johnson Why was that?
Ferris Don't ask *me*!

A pause

Johnson I thought you were the manager.
Ferris No. Just standing in for my sister.
Johnson Oh—yes...

A pause

Is she the one in Benidorm?
Ferris Yes!

A pause

Johnson So you're the *acting* manager?
Ferris Yes.

A pause

Johnson Why don't you know what's going on, then?

Henry comes in, urgently, from the main entrance

Henry Ferris! (*He sees them sitting together*) I'm not interrupting anything, am I?

Ferris gets up and goes to him

Ferris I thought you were leaving!
Henry My car won't start.
Ferris Did you push it?
Henry How can I push and drive at the same time? *You*'ll have to help me. (*He grabs Ferris by the arm*)
Ferris (*freeing himself*) I can't do that! I've got a bad back.
Henry But if I can't start my car I'll have to *stay* here!
Ferris That's all right. You can sleep on the sofa.
Henry Ferris! If I stay here my friend's husband is going to kill me!
Ferris You should have thought of that before you came here! Haven't angry husbands caught you with their wives before?
Henry (*horrified*) No! I've never done this before!
Ferris Well, now you'll never do it again!

Mr Johnson utters a low moan. They look at him

Henry Why is Mr Johnson still here?
Ferris He won't be for long. Your friend's husband is going to kill *him* as well.
Henry (*cheering up*) Oh, good! Then I can have *his* room?
Ferris No, you can't! She and Edgar are already in it.

The desk phone rings. They jump off the ground in unison. Ferris goes to answer it. Lights up in the Pink Room. Angela is on the phone, sitting in the armchair

Angela Ferris! You never gave it to me!
Ferris Never gave it to you? (*He looks at Henry and raises his eyebrows*)
Angela A slice of lemon! Remember? To go with my gin-and-tonic?

Ferris Ah—yes—a slice of lemon. Right away, miss. (*He is about to hang up*)
Angela And Ferris…!

Ferris lowers his ear to where the receiver is now

Ferris Yes, miss?
Angela More gin.
Ferris More gin, yes. (*He is about to hang up again*)
Angela And Ferris…!

Ferris's head is now almost on the desk in order to reach the phone

Ferris Yes, miss?
Angela On the double! (*She hangs up*)
Ferris A double on the double. Right! (*He succeeds in hanging up this time, and hastens away to get a bottle of gin and a slice of lemon on a stick*) She's drinking rather heavily. I think it's going to be a rough night. (*He starts to go towards the R stairs*) Look after Mr Johnson till I get back!
Henry Look after him? How?
Ferris I dunno! Take him for a walk in the garden! Show him the petunias.

Ferris goes at speed

Henry Oh—right. (*He goes to Mr Johnson*) Come on, then! (*He pulls him to his feet*)
Johnson Where are we going?
Henry Into the garden, apparently.
Johnson But I'm not feeling very well.
Henry You need a breath of fresh air!

Henry leads Mr Johnson out to the main entrance

In the Pink Room, Angela is sitting, patiently waiting for gin. A knock at the door

Angela Come in!

Ferris comes in and goes to her

Ferris One slice of lemon, Miss Forward. (*He drops the slice of lemon into her glass, delicately this time. He notices the level of her drink*) Should I freshen you up a little?

Angela (*enthusiastically*) Oh, yes, I think you should!

Ferris pours a little gin and then stops. Angela reaches out and guides his hand into pouring a larger measure. Ferris giggles with slight remonstration

Ferris Oh, Miss Forward!
Angela Don't worry. You can put it on my bill.
Ferris Oh, *no*, miss—please—your gin is on the house. (*He smiles, sycophantically*)
Angela Is it really?
Ferris Of course! (*He starts to go with the bottle*)
Angela In that case you may as well leave the bottle.
Ferris Leave the bottle—yes—right. (*Dutifully, he puts the bottle down on the table beside her*)
Angela Thank you, Ferris.
Ferris (*with a little chuckle*) He didn't hang about, did he?
Angela Who?
Ferris Your friend downstairs.
Angela Oh, Edgar! No, he didn't...
Ferris Dashed off into the garden as though the devil was after him. Bit of a surprise, was it? Running into each other like that?
Angela Yes, it certainly was...! I haven't seen him for years.
Ferris Bit odd, though, not wanting to stay and have a chat. Still, perhaps he wanted a breath of fresh air before getting down to the nitty-gritty. I'm sure he'll be back soon to catch up on old times.
Angela (*quietly*) I hope he won't...!
Ferris So I'll leave you with your gin, then, Miss Forward. Nothing like a bit of Dutch courage, eh? (*He laughs a little and makes a dive for the door*)
Angela Ferris...!

Ferris puts on the brakes. Angela gets up and goes towards him

Do you have *another* name?
Ferris Sorry?
Angela Well, we can't go on calling you Ferris, can we?
Ferris Can't we?
Angela Ferris is so unfriendly. And we don't want to be unfriendly, do we? What's your first name?

Ferris hesitates

Ferris Er ... well...
Angela Oh, come on—tell me...

Ferris plucks up courage

Ferris Francis.
Angela (*clapping her hands together delightedly*) Francis Ferris! How nice!
Ferris Thank you, miss. (*He dives for the door again*)
Angela Francis!

Ferris stops again

Perhaps I'll have it in my room tonight.
Ferris W-What would that be?
Angela Dinner!
Ferris (*relieved*) Oh, that—yes...
Angela You do have room service?
Ferris Oh, yes, miss! Of course! With pleasure.
Angela Room service *and* pleasure? What a combination!
Ferris I'll get the menu. (*He makes another dive for the door*)
Angela Francis...!

And again he has to stop

How long is your sister away for?
Ferris Until Thursday.
Angela (*with a suggestive smile*) Oh, good! We've got plenty of time, then.
Ferris I'll get the menu! (*He darts away again and succeeds in opening the door*)
Angela Don't leave me long, will you?

Ferris races out, closing the door behind him

Angela chuckles, enjoying his discomfort, and goes into the bathroom as the Lights go out in the Pink Room

In the reception area, Mr Johnson comes back in from the garden with Henry pursuing him

Henry That wasn't much of a walk!
Johnson Well, it's not much of a garden! I'd rather sit down. I'm not feeling very well. (*He sits down on the sofa again*)

Ferris staggers down the R stairs and goes to find the menu

Henry goes to him anxiously

Henry Are you all right, Ferris? You look quite pale.

Ferris I'm not surprised! She's had a lot to drink and she's getting very persistent.

Henry You should be pleased. That's what you wanted, isn't it?

Ferris No fear!

Henry But your sister wants the hotel to have a good report in the Sunday newspaper, doesn't she?

Ferris Yes, but——

Henry So if it makes Miss Forward happy, you'll have to give her what she wants.

Ferris (*appalled*) I can't do that!

Henry Why? What *does* she want?

Ferris The menu.

Henry Is *that* all?

Ferris No! That's just for starters! Then she wants room service and pleasure.

Henry In that order?

Ferris No—both together!

Mr Johnson emits a long, gentle moan. Ferris looks at him in surprise

What's *he* doing here? I told you to take him into the garden.

Henry He didn't like the look of your petunias.

Johnson I think I'm going to be sick…

Ferris and Henry exchange a look of alarm and hasten across to Mr Johnson

Ferris I *told* you not to eat stale sandwiches! Now see what's happened! (*To Henry*) This is *all* I need. Miss Forward will write in her newspaper that all the guests were throwing up after lunch!

Henry Give him some brandy. That'll settle his stomach.

Ferris I'm not wasting brandy on *him*!

Henry Give him an indigestion tablet, then!

Ferris looks at him, appalled by such a suggestion

Ferris An indigestion tablet? We don't have indigestion tablets here! This is a hotel, not a medical centre.

Henry Well, have a look! You never know. Maybe your sister has trouble with her tummy.

Ferris gives him a weary look and goes to the desk to search frantically for indigestion tablets

Ferris The chef wouldn't be very pleased if he thought we kept indigestion tablets to hand out to the guests after dinner. (*He finds some and is surprised*) Good heavens! There *are* some! (*He holds up the tablets*)

Henry You see? Your poor sister must have been suffering in silence for years.

Ferris Well, for God's sake, don't tell the chef. He's temperamental enough as it is. You fetch a glass of water. Let's hope one of these will do the trick.

Ferris takes one of the pills out of the packet as Henry gets a glass of water from the trolley. They go to Mr Johnson and—to his surprise—pull him to his feet, one on either side of him

Right! Here you are, Mr Johnson! (*He holds out the pill*)

Mr Johnson looks at the pill blankly for a moment

Johnson Is it a suicide pill?

Ferris I wish it *was*...! Of course it's not a suicide pill! It's an indigestion tablet.

Johnson I'd rather have a brandy.

Henry I told you he would.

Ferris It'll stop you feeling sick. Come on—open your mouth!

Johnson No! I won't! (*He closes his mouth firmly*)

Ferris Just put the pill on the back of your tongue——

Henry (*in similar rhythm*) And chase it down with the water!

They proffer the pill and the water, but Mr Johnson keeps his mouth tight shut and makes negative noises, shaking his head the while

Ferris You don't want to go on feeling sick, do you?

Mr Johnson shakes his head

Then open your mouth and swallow the pill!

The old man shakes his head again, his mouth still tightly buttoned

Henry It's no good. He won't do it.

Ferris Well, hold his nose! That should do the trick.

Reluctantly, Henry holds on to Mr Johnson's nose, causing the old man's eyes to dilate. Ferris grabs his chin and tries to open his mouth. A small struggle ensues. Without success. So they give that up and the old man breathes freely again

Henry *Now* what are we going to do?

Ferris You tell him a joke. That'll make him laugh. Then he'll *have* to open his mouth.

Henry I don't know any jokes…

Ferris Not even one?

Henry Well … only one. And I'm not sure if it's funny.

Ferris Then try it on *me* first!

They bend towards each other, leaning on Mr Johnson, and Henry whispers soundlessly in Ferris's ear. It is quite a long story, and Ferris starts to laugh halfway through. When the silent story ends Ferris is impressed

That's very good!

Ferris and Henry laugh heartily—and continuously! Mr Johnson is puzzled by their levity. As their laughter proceeds, Ferris pushes Mr Johnson playfully from one side, then Henry does the same from the other side. Mr Johnson begins to find that their laughter is infectious. He tries to control himself, but fails to do so. He begins to smile—little by little—then suddenly and noisily joins in their riotous laughter—opening his mouth wide in the process! Ferris pops the pill into Mr Johnson's open mouth, and Henry follows up with the water, spilling some in the process. But the old man has swallowed the pill, and looks surprised at what has occurred. Henry puts down the glass of water while Ferris (having palmed the pill) mops up the spillage with a cloth, and tidies up Mr Johnson generally

There! That wasn't very difficult, was it?

Johnson *(recovering)* Now can I have some brandy?

Ferris *(relenting)* Oh, all right, then. But you'll have to have it in the lounge! *(He pushes Mr Johnson towards the lounge and turns back to Henry)* I'm going to have my hands full with *him*—so *you*'ll have to see to Miss Forward! *(He thrusts the menu at him)*

Henry No fear, Ferris!

Ferris All you have to do is to show her the menu and ask her what she wants.

Henry You've already told me what she wants! And she's not getting it from me.

Ferris You wouldn't want Edgar to find out about you and his wife, would you?

Henry *(appalled)* You wouldn't *tell* him?

Ferris I might. You never know.

Henry But, Ferris—that's blackmail!

Ferris Is it? Oh. Yes, I suppose it is. *(He grins broadly)* Anyway, you did say you were a man who'd like to help in an emergency.

Henry Is that what *this* is?

Ferris Didn't you realize?
Henry No. Oh, well, in that case I suppose I'll *have* to… (*He takes the menu*)
Ferris (*gratefully*) Thank you, sir!
Henry Thank *you*, Ferris! (*He holds out his hand, pointedly*)

Reluctantly, Ferris gives him some more money

   Henry smiles triumphantly, pockets the money and goes out up the R stairs

Ferris goes quickly back to Mr Johnson

Ferris Right! Off we go! You'll feel better now you've had that pill.
Johnson I'll feel better when I've had the brandy!

   Ferris and Mr Johnson go into the lounge

   Edgar comes in from the garden, looking about furtively. Seeing that all is clear he goes quickly up the L stairs

Lights up in the Blue Room

   Edgar comes in as Judy comes out of the bathroom. He is in a bit of a state, which she notices

Judy Whatever's the matter?
Edgar (*abruptly*) What?!
Judy Are you all right?
Edgar Yes! Yes!
Judy (*aside*) He doesn't seem all right. (*To Edgar*) You don't seem all right.
Edgar A bit breathless. There are a lot of stairs.
Judy (*an alarming thought*) You didn't *do* it, did you?
Edgar Do it?
Judy What you *said* you were going to do.
Edgar What was that?
Judy (*aside*) How can he have forgotten? (*To Edgar*) How can you have forgotten? You were going to kill somebody.
Edgar Ah—yes—I *had* forgotten.
Judy (*shocked*) Forgotten a thing like that?!
Edgar I had more important matters on my mind…
Judy More important than killing the owner of a suitcase?
Edgar He was an old man!
Judy So why are you in such a state? (*Anxiously*) You haven't found something out, have you?

Edgar No! Nothing at all! No!
Judy Perhaps you'll feel better after dinner, dear.
Edgar Dinner?!

Judy is puzzled by his vehemence about dinner

Judy You *said* you wanted dinner.
Edgar I'm not hungry any more!
Judy Well, *I* am…
Edgar You can send for room service.
Judy I'd rather eat in the dining-room.
Edgar No! I'll speak to the manager!
Judy What about?
Edgar You were right. This room is too small for two people. I'll tell him
to find me another room.
Judy (*trying to hide her pleasure*) Really? Oh—right. If you're sure, Edgar.
Edgar Then I can have room service and you can eat in the dining-room. (*He
hastens to the door*)
Judy (*puzzled*) Are you *sure* you're all right?
Edgar Yes! Yes—fine! Definitely! Fine! (*As he goes*) Oh, my God…

Edgar exits, shutting the door behind him

Judy I wish now that I'd stayed at home and watched the telly…

Judy goes into the bathroom

*Lights out in the Blue Room as the Lights come up in the Pink Room. A knock
at the door*

*Angela comes out of the bathroom and goes to open the door, expecting it
to be Ferris*

Henry is there with the menu

Angela I wasn't expecting *you*!
Henry No, I know, but——
Angela You can't come back in here! This is *my* room now. Didn't he tell
you?
Henry (*nervously*) I—I believe you wanted room service.
Angela Yes. But I didn't think *you* were going to give it to me. You're not
a member of staff. Where's Francis?
Henry Who?
Angela Mr Ferris!

Henry Is that his name? Francis? (*He laughs*)

Angela Why isn't *he* here? He is supposed to be the deputy manager.

Henry They're short-staffed, so I ... volunteered.

Angela Volunteered?

Henry To give a hand.

Angela Have you had any experience?

Henry Sorry?

Angela Of giving service in the bedroom!

Henry Ah—no. I'm afraid not.

Angela You might not be able to do it.

Henry Well ... I brought the menu. (*He holds out the menu to her*)

Angela That's a start, I suppose. (*She sits down and looks at the menu*) Why
don't you pour me another gin while I'm making up my mind?

Henry Gin. Right. (*He starts to replenish her drink*) Say when.

Angela does not say when, so he continues pouring

Did you say it?

Angela What?

Henry When.

Angela Oh. (*A beat*) When.

Henry stops pouring, by which time the glass is very full indeed

(*Admiringly*) At least you know how to pour gin. (*She sips her large gin*)
Is your lady friend still crying?

Henry I wouldn't be surprised.

Angela Won't she be wondering where you are?

Henry I shouldn't think so...

Angela Why not?

Henry Because her husband's turned up!

Angela He hasn't!

Henry He has!

Angela Well—that *is* a coincidence. So has mine!

Henry (*alarmed*) What?!

They freeze. Lights out in the Pink Room

*In the reception area, Edgar is coming quickly down the L stairs as Ferris
comes out of the lounge and sees him*

Ferris Everything all right, sir?

Edgar (*jumping*) What?

Ferris You're happy with your wife's room?
Edgar No, I am not!
Ferris Oh, dear. What a pity.
Edgar She was right. It *is* a bit small.
Ferris Sorry?
Edgar My wife's room! It's too small for two. *I* shall have to sleep elsewhere.
Ferris But there is no elsewhere!
Edgar No elsewhere?
Ferris Elsewhere is occupied. Didn't you book a room of your own?
Edgar No. I came here on the off-chance. So you're going to have to find one for me!
Ferris Oh, I can't do that. All the rooms are taken.
Edgar Ferris—I'm an angry man when I'm roused. You wouldn't like to rouse me, would you?
Ferris No! Certainly not!

Edgar glances around anxiously

Edgar Where would I find the ... the other lady?
Ferris Other lady?
Edgar The one who came downstairs looking for lemon.
Ferris Oh—*that* lady! Yes, it is time you had a word with her. She must be wondering where you went to. Bit of a surprise, was it, finding her here?
Edgar Yes. It was! We haven't seen each other for years.
Ferris You didn't seem very pleased to see her, though. Took one look and darted out into the garden. Mr Johnson and I were *very* surprised.
Edgar I ... I wasn't feeling very well. Had a bit of a turn.
Ferris That's what I thought! Exactly what I said to Mr Johnson. I expect he's had a bit of a turn, I said. Still, now you've had a breath of fresh air you can have a nice long chat before dinner.
Edgar (*anxiously*) Will she be eating in the dining-room?
Ferris Oh, no. I think she prefers the privacy of the boudoir. (*He closes to him; inquisitively*) Were you two—you know—close?
Edgar No! We were not!
Ferris Lucky for you, eh? Would have been a bit embarrassing, wouldn't it, if you *had* been? Your wife being here and all that.
Edgar We were good friends! Nothing more!
Ferris Well, you'd better go and say hullo, then. She's in Number Four. The honeymoon suite.
Edgar Honeymoon? You mean she's here on...?
Ferris Oh, no! Nothing like that. It's just that—under the circumstances— I wanted her to have the best room in the hotel.
Edgar What circumstances?

Ferris Oh, I can't tell you that! I think she wants it kept a secret.
Edgar A secret, eh? I see... All right. Thank you, Ferris!
Ferris Thank *you*, sir. (*He starts to go*)
Edgar Ferris!

Ferris returns at once

Ferris There! I wasn't away long, was I?
Edgar Remember what I want!
Ferris I think I've forgotten what it is...
Edgar A room! A room! Study the register!
Ferris Study the register. I will! I will! (*He starts to go again*)
Edgar And Ferris...!

Ferris returns at once

Ferris Here I am again, sir!
Edgar No need to mention to my wife that there's someone here that I used to know. Don't want her jumping to conclusions.
Ferris Of course not, sir! My lips are sealed. (*He holds out his hand*)

Edgar glares at him, but for safety's sake gives him some money. Ferris expresses extreme surprise

Oh, *thank* you, sir! What a kind thought.

Ferris darts out into the kitchen

Edgar glares after Ferris's departing figure and goes out up the R stairs

Lights up in the Pink Room. Henry prepares to go

Henry I'll leave you to it, then.
Angela But you haven't taken my order!
Henry I'm not staying here!
Angela Why are you so nervous? Your crying friend's not going to be looking for you now that her husband's arrived.
Henry It's not *her* husband I'm worried about!

A knock at the door

Ah! That'll be him!
Angela Who?

Henry Your husband!
Angela No, no! It'll only be Francis.
Henry Is he a jealous man?
Angela Francis?
Henry Your husband!
Angela (*trying to remember*) Yes. I think so...
Henry Violently jealous?
Angela Well, he used to be.
Henry Used to be?! If he was violent once he'll be violent again!

Another loud knock on the door

Oh, my God! What'll happen if he finds *me* here?
Angela What does it matter? You're a member of staff. Here to take my order for room service. (*She goes towards the door*)
Henry *He*'s not going to believe that, though, is he?

Henry darts out into the bathroom and shuts the door

Angela opens the door to the corridor

Edgar is there

They stare at each other, just as Edgar and Judy did earlier

Angela (*with a smile*) Edgar...!
Edgar (*without a smile*) Angela...!

Edgar comes in. Angela closes the door. They face each other again

Angela...
Angela Edgar...
Edgar Well, at least we know who we are. I suppose I ought to embrace you.
Angela Why?
Edgar I am your husband. I *used* to embrace you.
Angela Very well. If you want to.

They embrace perfunctorily

Edgar (*aside*) This *is* a surprise...!
Angela (*aside*) What's he doing here?

They come out of their embrace

Edgar This *is* a surprise!

Angela What are you doing here?

Edgar I *must* talk to you!

Angela (*with a smile*) You didn't seem very keen to talk to me downstairs. You took one look and galloped off into the garden!

Edgar Yes. Sorry. I was on the back foot. Needed time to focus. Now, the thing is——

Angela Why did you never divorce me?

Edgar What?!

Angela I *was* the guilty party, after all. Did you never want to marry again?

Edgar (*vehemently*) No! *Never!*

Angela Oh, Edgar... I'm quite touched. So what are you here for?

Edgar Business! I'm here on business!

Angela Are you alone?

Edgar Yes! Yes! Are *you*?

Angela Yes.

A window bangs shut in the bathroom

Edgar No, you're not! There's somebody in the bathroom!

Angela No!

Edgar I heard a noise!

Angela Yes. The window blowing shut!

Edgar After a departing lover? That's where wives hide their lovers, isn't it? In the bathroom? If you've got a man in there I'll kill him!

Angela (*as if to a child*) But Edgar—it's nothing to do with you. We don't live together any more.

Edgar Maybe not. But I'm still a jealous husband. (*He goes to the bathroom*)

Angela It'll be the chambermaid! I asked her to see to the soap.

Edgar opens the bathroom door abruptly and goes inside

Angela awaits the inevitable explosion

But Edgar returns, puzzled

Edgar There's nobody there.

Angela Are you sure?

Edgar If the chambermaid *was* in there, she must have jumped out of the window.

Angela But we're on the second floor! (*She goes towards the bathroom*)

Edgar has noticed something

Edgar I thought so! You *have* been entertaining someone!

Angela (*stopping*) What?

Edgar (*going to it*) There's a bottle of champagne! And *two* glasses! You said you were here alone!

Angela I *am* alone!

Edgar (*with dark suspicion*) Alone in the honeymoon suite? Ferris told me you had a secret. So that's what he meant. You're meeting a man here!

Angela No, Edgar. I'm not. But what if I was? (*She pats his face gently*) It's none of your business. (*Then, puzzled*) Are you *sure* the chambermaid isn't in there?

Angela goes into the bathroom to look

Edgar starts to follow her, suitably reprimanded

Edgar (*going*) Angela, there's something I *must* talk to you about...!

Lights out in the Pink Room

In the reception area, Henry staggers in from the garden. His clothes are dishevelled, his hair untidy and he is breathing heavily

Ferris comes in from the kitchen. He sees this apparition and laughs

Ferris I didn't realize that Miss Forward was going to be as forward as all that!

Henry *She* didn't do this!

Ferris What have you been up to, then?

Henry I've been climbing down a drainpipe.

Ferris You were supposed to be taking her order for room service, not practising mountain climbing!

Henry I was outside her bathroom window and the only way to escape was down the drainpipe.

Ferris What on earth were you doing outside her bathroom window?

Henry Hiding!

Ferris Hiding from Miss Forward?

Henry No! From somebody *else*! She had a man up there!

Ferris laughs, enjoying the situation

Ferris Yes—I know! Didn't you see who it was?

Henry No fear! I left before he came in!

Ferris (*quietly*) Thank God for that!

Henry It's not funny, Ferris!

Ferris It would have been if you'd seen him!

Henry Why? Do you know who it was?

Ferris Yes. It was your lady friend's husband!

Henry Edgar?!

Ferris Yes.

Henry What was *he* doing up there?

Ferris Catching up on old times. They came face-to-face with each other when you were trying to start your car. And they were very surprised to see each other. (*With heavy innuendo*) They're "old friends", apparently. (*He laughs*)

Henry No, Ferris! This man wasn't Edgar.

Ferris How do *you* know if you didn't see him?

Henry Because Miss Forward told me who he was! That's why I was hiding.

Ferris tries to comprehend

Ferris You mean there was *another* man up there? As *well* as Edgar?

Henry There must have been. Because this man wasn't an "old friend". This was her *husband*!

Ferris Miss Forward's husband?

Henry Yes!

Ferris (*puzzled*) She didn't say anything to *me* about a husband. When did *he* arrive, then?

Henry Just now, apparently!

Ferris Good heavens! *Two* husbands turning up unexpectedly! It'll soon be like a French farce.

Mr Johnson comes in from the lounge. He has acquired quite a spring in his step and a general air of dreamy self-confidence. He grins at them saucily as he circles the area, looking about

Feeling better, Mr Johnson?

Johnson Oh … yes! And now I'm ready for action! (*He giggles, gives a little skip and moves on*)

Ferris (*to Henry*) What the hell's happened to him? (*He goes to Mr Johnson*) I ordered your taxi. It should be here soon.

Mr Johnson waves a hand at Ferris dismissively

Johnson I don't want a taxi!

Ferris Yes, you do. You're leaving!

Johnson Don't have to leave if I don't want to. I may stay … a little longer … or a lot longer … if I want to…

Ferris But you can't stay now! Your room's full of other people.

Mr Johnson looks around the room hopefully

Johnson Where are the ladies? I don't see any sign of the ladies…

Ferris and Henry turn to each other

Ferris ⎫
Henry ⎬ (*together*) Ladies?!

Henry Whatever did we give him?
Ferris Only a pill for indigestion.
Henry Are you *sure* that's what it was for?
Ferris Well, that's what I *thought* it was for…! (*He realizes and looks at Henry in horror*) Oh, my God! You don't think it was…?
Henry (*nodding*) Yes! It must have been for something else…!
Ferris Just look at the state of him!

Mr Johnson is revolving slowly

Johnson Where have you hidden the ladies…?
Ferris (*to Henry*) My sister would never have something like that! Mind you, she has got a rather elderly husband…
Henry That's it, then!
Ferris Oh, my God…!

Mr Johnson starts to head optimistically towards the L stairs. Ferris sees him

He's heading for the stairs!

They run after Mr Johnson, take one arm each, lift him up, and carry him back again

Not up there, Mr Johnson! You don't belong up there any more.
Johnson Don't be such a spoilsport! (*He escapes and goes towards the stairs again*)

Ferris and Henry pursue him once again, take one arm each, lift him up and carry him back again

Ferris No, Mr Johnson! You're not to go up there.
Johnson (*sulking*) Your sister would let me go if *she* was here…
Ferris No, she wouldn't!
Henry (*to Ferris*) What are you going to do with him?

Ferris We'll put him back in the lounge.

Mr Johnson sets off again at speed for the stairs

Henry He's off again!

Ferris and Henry race after him yet again, and carry him back as before

Ferris You won't find the ladies up there, Mr Johnson. (*Lying desperately*) The ladies are in the lounge.
Johnson (*wisely*) They weren't in the lounge a moment ago...
Henry (*helpfully*) No—they were in the dining-room *then*. Weren't they, Ferris?
Ferris (*catching on*) Ah—yes! Yes—they were—and *now* they've gone into the lounge.
Johnson (*his eyes lighting up*) Really? Oh, good!

Mr Johnson trots off into the lounge, smiling optimistically

Ferris and Henry shake hands

Henry You'd better get him some black coffee. See if that'll sober him up a bit.
Ferris I'm sure my sister never had trouble like this. *And* I've got to find another bedroom for Edgar!
Henry Isn't he moving in with Judy?
Ferris No. He wants a room on his own. (*Suddenly realizing*) Ah! So that's all right, then, isn't it?
Henry (*puzzled*) What's all right, then?
Ferris If he's having a room on his own you don't have to sleep on this sofa. You can go back in with your lady friend.
Henry (*appalled*) I can't do that!
Ferris Why not?
Henry It ... it would be dangerous.
Ferris (*as if to a child*) If you go away with married women it's bound to be dangerous!
Henry Yes. I ... I suppose so...
Ferris Go on, then! She's in Number Twelve. (*He gives Henry an encouraging push*)

After a few steps, Henry turns back

Henry Are you sure I'm doing the right thing?
Ferris If you want to be a ladies' man you'll have to learn to live dangerously.

Henry Right! I'll do it!

Henry goes up the L stairs

Ferris grins. Then he hesitates uncertainly

Ferris Now, what's next? Ah, yes—coffee for Mr Johnson!

Ferris hastens into the kitchen

Lights up in the Pink Room

Angela is coming out of the bathroom

Angela I can't think *what*'s happened to the chambermaid...

Edgar follows her from the bathroom

Edgar Angela, I must talk to you!
Angela Well, you can't stay here! I'm going to have a bath.
Edgar I came to ask you a favour! Well? Will you do it?
Angela You haven't said what it is yet.

Edgar glances around, then closes to her, confidentially

Edgar Don't let anyone know that we used to be married.
Angela We're *still* married.
Edgar Yes. I know. But we don't want to tell everyone, do we?
Angela Oh, Edgar! Are you ashamed of me?
Edgar No, no! But there are ... people here.
Angela Of course there are. It's a hotel.
Edgar People who know me! And these ... people ... don't know that I'm married.
Angela What people?
Edgar (*irritably*) What does it matter what people? People!
Angela What sort of people?
Edgar Business people!
Angela Business people who wouldn't approve of you being married? Whatever sort of business are they in?
Edgar (*trying to be patient*) Just pretend that we're old friends...
Angela We *are* old friends. (*With a smile*) Old *married* friends...
Edgar Well, pretend that we're *not* married!
Angela Oh, all right, Edgar. If it's so important.

Edgar (*gratefully*) Thank you, Angela! (*He starts to go, then looks back with exaggerated warmth*) I'm *so* glad to see you again.

Edgar goes, closing the door behind him

Angela reacts to this and then hastens into the bathroom to find out what has happened to Henry

Lights out in the Pink Room

In the reception area, Edgar runs down the R stairs

Ferris!

No sign of him

Ferris!

Edgar goes into the lounge

Lights up in the Blue Room. Someone knocks on the door

Judy comes out of the bathroom nervously and goes to open the door

Henry is there

She glares at him

Judy What are *you* doing here?
Henry I'm living dangerously. (*He walks in, smiling confidently*)

Judy shuts the door and follows him

Judy You certainly are! My husband's in the hotel!
Henry That's all right, pigeon. He won't be coming back in *here*! Ferris is finding him another room.
Judy Well, that doesn't mean that *you* can come in here!
Henry Doesn't it? Why not?
Judy Because *you*'ve got yourself another woman!
Henry No!
Judy Then how do you explain *her* bag on *our* bed? *And* with a frilly night-dress inside! (*Unhappily*) I can't compete with that sort of thing...
Henry It was a mistake...!

Judy She was sipping our champagne and waiting for *you!* (*Her face crumbling*) And all because I was a little late arriving...!

Henry No, pigeon...!

Judy It was the taxi driver's fault, not mine! He should have known the way. *They*'re the ones who are paid to know the way, not the passengers! (*She cries loudly*)

Henry But she *wasn't* waiting for me! I came here to be with *you*, not with somebody else.

So Judy allows her crying to cease

Judy Did you?

Henry Of course!

Judy (*suitably mollified*) Oh—well, that's all right, then. (*She smiles happily, then has another thought*) It's not very flattering, though, is it?

Henry What isn't?

Judy My husband not wanting to sleep in the same room as me.

Henry (*after considering this for a moment*) Yes... I see what you mean. I hadn't thought of that. It is a bit insulting...

Judy Maybe *he*'s got an assignation...

Henry Edgar?!

Judy Yes. Perhaps *he*'s doing what I was doing! Perhaps he came here to meet another woman when I was coming here to meet another man...

Henry But in that case he'd have booked a room, wouldn't he? Like I did. He wouldn't have just turned up on the off-chance.

Judy No, I suppose not. And he did say he was here on business...

Henry (*reassuringly*) Well, there you are, then! He doesn't want to sleep with you because it would take his mind *off* his business. So that *is* flattering, isn't it?

Judy Yes! Of course it is! Why didn't *I* think of that?

Henry So that's all right, then, isn't it?

Judy (*puzzled*) What is?

Henry If Edgar's going to sleep somewhere else—*we* can carry on from where we left off.

Judy (*thinking deeply*) I can't remember where that was...

Henry Neither can I...

They sit on the end of the bed and try to remember. Lights out in the Blue Room

In the reception area, Angela comes down the R stairs as Ferris comes out of the kitchen with a pot of coffee and a mug

Angela Have you seen him anywhere?

Ferris Who?

Angela Your "volunteer" waiter! The one you sent to take my order. He went into the bathroom and disappeared. I'm quite worried about him.

Ferris Oh! You don't have to worry about Just Henry. He found a very good drainpipe.

Angela He descended from my bathroom down a *drainpipe*?

Ferris I think he used to be in the SAS.

Angela And where is he now?

Ferris Oh, he's busy giving service in another room now. (*He laughs saucily*)

Angela That's all right, then. So now I shall go and have a bath. (*She starts to go*)

Ferris A bath? I thought you and Edgar were catching up on old times.

Angela No. He left in rather a hurry. He had *other* things on his mind.

Ferris (*quietly*) Yes. I'm sure he did...! (*He sidles near to her, playfully*) You never told me you had a husband arriving. I always think of you as Miss Forward. I was quite surprised.

Angela So was I...! There is one thing, though, Francis.

Ferris Anything you say, Miss Forward! Your wish is our command.

Angela Please don't mention about my husband to anyone else.

Ferris (*appalled at the idea of such an indiscretion*) My lips are sealed! In this hotel we know how to be discreet...

Angela Thank you, Francis! (*She starts to go*)

Ferris Thank *you*, miss. (*He starts to hold out his hand, hoping for a tip, then hastily abandons the idea, deeming it to be inappropriate*) Would you like me to run your bath for you, miss—er—madam?

Angela (*with a smile*) Thank you, Francis. But I think I can manage. (*She starts to go again*)

Ferris (*quietly*) Yes. I'm sure you can...

Angela (*looking back at him*) And then I shall be requiring room service!

Ferris I thought you might...

Angela And this time, Francis—I'd prefer *you* to give it to me.

Ferris I'll do my best... I take it that'll be for *two*?

Angela Certainly not! I'm dining alone.

Angela goes back up the R stairs

Ferris (*calling after her*) But what about your *husband*?

But she has gone

Edgar pounds in from the lounge

Edgar Ferris!

Ferris jumps, nearly spilling the coffee

Ferris *Now* see what you've done! I nearly spilt the coffee. (*He grins cheekily*) *You* didn't have much of a chat, did you?
Edgar Chat? What chat?
Ferris With your friend in the honeymoon suite!
Edgar Ah—no. No, she—er—she wanted to have a bath. And you were right, Ferris. She *did* have a secret!

Ferris is surprised by this revelation

Ferris You mean she *told* you why she was here?
Edgar She didn't have to tell me, did she? I knew! (*He leans in to Ferris confidentially*) He must have climbed out of the window.

Ferris is obviously rather confused by this

Ferris Ah—yes… (*He tries to work this out*)
Edgar Ferris!

Ferris jumps again

Ferris (*indicating the coffee pot*) See? I nearly did it again!
Edgar Have you done that which you ought to have done?
Ferris Sorry?
Edgar You were preventing me from being roused by finding me another room!
Ferris Ah. Yes. I knew there was something. And luckily there's just been a cancellation. Just a moment ago. So now you can have Number Seventeen. In the garden. Overlooking the car park.
Edgar The car park? Is that an advantage?
Ferris It is if you want to leave in a hurry.
Edgar Right! I'll fetch my bag.
Ferris What?!
Edgar I can't move in without my bag. I shall need my toothbrush.
Ferris You're not going to brush your teeth *now*, are you?
Edgar I always brush my teeth before dinner. And my toothbrush is in my bag.
Ferris And where did you leave your bag?
Edgar In my wife's room, of course!
Ferris Oh, no…!
Edgar Is that a problem?
Ferris Yes…!

Edgar What?
Ferris No!
Edgar Right. I'll go and fetch it, then. (*He starts to go*)
Ferris No!

Edgar stops, surprised by Ferris's vehemence

Edgar You said it wasn't a problem.
Ferris No, but *I*'ll fetch it! I am the deputy manager, after all.
Edgar But I wish to speak to my wife.
Ferris I can give her a message! And that would save you carrying your bag.
Edgar It's a very small bag. I think I can manage a very small bag. Anyway, you're busy taking coffee to someone, aren't you? (*He indicates the coffee pot that Ferris is carrying*)
Ferris I'd forgotten all about him!
Edgar Right. Then I'll get my bag.

Edgar goes up the L stairs

Ferris I hope he remembers to knock...

Mr Johnson comes in from the lounge

Johnson I can't find them!
Ferris Who?
Johnson The ladies!
Ferris Never mind the ladies! I've brought you coffee.

Ferris leads the way back into the lounge

Johnson (*following*) I don't want coffee! I want *women*...!

Mr Johnson goes out after Ferris

Lights up in the Blue Room. Henry and Judy are sitting as before, deep in thought. Henry activates himself

Henry Ah! I remember!
Judy Do you?
Henry Surely you haven't forgotten why I asked you to come here?
Judy Oh, that! Yes, I remember that. (*Shyly*) You said you wanted to sleep with me...
Henry Yes.

Judy I don't think I could *get* to sleep now...

Henry (*smiling hopefully*) Why don't you go and lock the door?

Judy I've never done this before, Henry. Is that the procedure? Lock the door first?

Henry Well, we don't want to be disturbed, do we?

Judy No. Not if we're fast asleep. What will *you* be doing while I'm locking the door?

Henry smiles sheepishly

Henry Well... I'll be taking my trousers off.

Judy Will you?

Henry Yes. It would be advisable.

They laugh self-consciously

Judy All right. I'll lock the door then. (*She goes to lock the door, and remains facing the door, her back to Henry*)

Henry starts to take off his trousers at speed. But he cannot get them over his shoes. So he panics. Naturally. And struggles

(*Still facing the door*) Have you done it yet?

Henry No—not yet! (*He keeps trying*)

A pause

Judy It's taking you a long time.

Henry Yes!

A pause

Judy Shall I give you a hand?

Henry No! (*He continues the struggle*)

A pause

Judy What exactly is the problem?

Henry I can't get my trousers over my shoes!

Judy turns and sees him struggling. And, not unnaturally, she laughs

It's not funny!

Judy Yes, it is! I never thought that being a femme fatale would be like this.

(*She watches his struggle for a moment*) Shouldn't you have taken your shoes off first?

Henry glares at her accusingly

Henry You've done this *before*, haven't you?
Judy No, of course not!
Henry Well, you're giving me a lot of advice about how to take my trousers off!
Judy It ... it just seemed to be common sense, that's all.
Henry Anyway, it's too late to do that now. I'm halfway there! You'll have to give me a hand.
Judy Well, I'll try. But I'm not used to helping gentlemen remove their trousers. (*She goes to him, and her nearness to his struggling makes her laugh again*) How am I supposed to start?
Henry (*furiously*) Oh, for heaven's sake—just pull!

Judy tentatively takes hold of his trousers and pulls. They struggle for a while. Finally, she succeeds in pulling off his trousers to reveal striped boxer shorts

And, of course, someone tries to open the bedroom door. They freeze in alarm

Judy (*in an urgent whisper*) There's someone trying to get in!
Henry It'll be Ferris.
Judy (*calling*) Is that you, Mr Ferris?
Edgar (*off*) No, it's not! It's me—Edgar!
Henry ⎱ (*together*) Edgar!
Judy ⎰
Henry Oh, my God...!
Judy I didn't think it would be like this—removing gentlemen's trousers and hiding from my husband! In future I think I'll stick to bingo.

More loud knocking on the door

Edgar (*off*) Judy! Come on! Open the door!
Judy (*calling*) Just a minute! (*To Henry, desperately*) Henry—what's the procedure for *this*?

Henry hastens towards the bathroom

Where are you going? You can't leave me here!
Henry It's all right—*I*'ve done this *before*...!

Henry darts out into the bathroom

Judy quickly tidies herself up and goes to open the door

Edgar comes in, looking about suspiciously

Edgar Why did you lock the door?
Judy I—I was going to have a bath.
Edgar I just came to fetch my bag. (*He goes to pick up his weekend bag*)

As he does this, Judy notices Henry's trousers on the end of the bed. She hastily grabs them and shoves them under the bed, unseen by Edgar, who is busy with his bag

Mr Ferris has found me another room.
Judy Oh, good!
Edgar What?
Judy Well, that's what you wanted, wasn't it?
Edgar So I'm going to move into Number Seventeen. In the garden. Overlooking the car park.

There is a sudden noise as Henry knocks something over in the bathroom

There's somebody in your bathroom!
Judy No!
Edgar Yes! I heard a noise!
Judy But there's nobody there!
Edgar I'm a very jealous husband!
Judy Yes—I know.
Edgar If you're hiding a man in there I'll kill him! (*He goes towards the bathroom*)
Judy It'll be the chambermaid!
Edgar (*having heard this before*) Chambermaid? You didn't ask her to see to the soap, by any chance?

Judy is grateful for the suggestion

Judy Yes! I did! However did you guess?

Edgar tries to open the bathroom door, but it is locked

Edgar Does the chambermaid usually lock the door when she's seeing to the soap?
Judy I suppose she likes to concentrate. Doesn't want to be disturbed...
Edgar I'll disturb her...! (*He goes decisively to the door*) I shall go and find Ferris.

Judy (*quietly*) Oh, good!
Edgar And then I shall be back!
Judy Oh, dear…!

Edgar goes, closing the door behind him abruptly

Judy runs to the bathroom door and knocks on it

Henry! It's all right—he's gone!

No reply from within. Which puzzles her

(*Calling*) Henry…! (*She tries the door*) Henry! Oh, no! Where can he have gone to? (*She remembers Henry's trousers are under the bed and runs back to retrieve them. She dithers for a moment, uncertain what to do*) Now what am I supposed to do…? I'm all alone in a hotel bedroom with an uninhabited pair of gentleman's trousers!

Then Judy starts to go

Lights out in the Blue Room

In the reception area, Mr Johnson is escaping from the lounge, pursued by Ferris with the coffee pot and mug

Johnson But I don't want coffee!
Ferris Yes, you do!
Johnson You lied to me, Mr Ferris! The ladies weren't out there at all! Where have you hidden them?
Ferris (*relenting*) Oh, all right, then. But I'll only tell you if you promise to have coffee first.
Johnson Then I'll have coffee first. (*He sits down on the sofa abruptly*)

Ferris pours him some coffee

Henry appears from the garden, a little dishevelled, breathless, and without his trousers

Ferris sees him, puts the coffee pot down on the sofa table, and goes across, amused by the spectacle

Ferris Oh, no! You haven't done it *again*? Say you haven't done it again!
Henry I've done it again…

Unseen by Ferris, Mr Johnson empties his mug of coffee into the nearby potted plant

Ferris (*laughing*) Didn't take you long to get your kit off, did it?
Henry Well, you told me to live dangerously.
Ferris *And* you managed to escape again!
Henry No. I'm still in the bathroom.
Ferris Sorry?
Henry Upstairs! The bathroom of Number Twelve! I'm still in there!
Ferris (*puzzled*) No, you're not. You're down here.
Henry But as far as *he*'s concerned I'm still up *there*!
Ferris Edgar?
Henry Yes!
Ferris Did he see you?
Henry No fear! I locked the door.
Ferris Did you take your trousers off before or after you went into the bathroom?
Henry Before, of course!
Ferris So your trousers are still in the bedroom?
Henry Yes!
Johnson (*looking at Henry*) I bet *you* know where the ladies are...

They turn to look at the source of the voice

Henry What?
Johnson Well, you aren't wearing any trousers.
Henry (*to Ferris*) He doesn't seem any better.
Ferris No, but at least he's drinking coffee. (*He goes to Mr Johnson*) Have you finished that, Mr Johnson? (*He sees the empty mug*) Oh, well done! You'd better have some more. (*He refills the mug*)
Johnson (*to Henry*) When I've had my coffee, Mr Ferris is going to tell me where he's hidden the ladies. (*He looks at his full mug of coffee dispiritedly*)
Henry Ferris!

Ferris returns to him

   I need your help!
Ferris Why? What have you done to yourself?
Henry Somebody's got to go back into that bathroom.
Ferris Your married lady friend's bathroom?
Henry Yes.
Ferris Why?
Henry Because Edgar won't give up until he gets the bathroom door open, and when he does he mustn't find *me*!

Ferris Why not?
Henry Because if he does he'll kill me!
Ferris Why can't he just find the bathroom empty?
Henry He knows someone was in there! And only a fool would climb out of a window two floors up.
Ferris *You* did! You did it twice.

Mr Johnson empties his coffee into the potted plant

Henry So it would be better when Edgar opens the bathroom door if he found somebody *else* there!
Ferris (*realizing what he is suggesting*) Oh, no! No—I won't do it! (*He tries to escape*)

Henry catches him and pulls him back

Henry I thought we were friends?
Ferris Not any more!
Henry You said we had to help each other in an emergency. I helped you with Angela. I even let her have the honeymoon suite.
Ferris Yes, I know, but...!
Henry Well, now it's *your* turn to help *me*!
Johnson Can we go and find the ladies now? (*He starts to get up*)

Ferris races across to Mr Johnson, and pushes him back on to the sofa

Ferris No! Not yet, Mr Johnson! (*He notices the again empty mug*) Good heavens! You've finished it again! (*To Henry*) He's got the most remarkable thirst. (*He refills the mug again and then goes back to Henry*)
Henry So that's all right, then?
Ferris No, it is *not* all right, then! If Edgar finds *me* in the bathroom, he'll kill me instead of you!
Henry Of course he won't.
Ferris Why not? I'll be hiding in his wife's bathroom! How's that going to look?
Henry But you're the acting manager. You can say you were seeing to the plumbing.
Ferris No! I won't do it! I'm not climbing up a drainpipe!
Henry You don't have to.
Ferris How's that?
Henry There's a little ledge outside Judy's bathroom window that leads along to the fire escape.
Ferris (*appalled*) A little ledge?!
Henry So all you have to do is go up the fire escape.

Ferris And along a little ledge!
Henry Well, *I* did it.
Ferris Yes, but you're the one who's in trouble!
Henry I'll make it worth your while.
Ferris How much worth?
Henry Five?
Ferris Ten.
Henry Done.

Ferris holds his hand out for the money. Henry remembers where his money is

    Ah. There is one snag.
Ferris I thought there might be.
Henry My trousers are in Judy's bedroom...
Ferris And your money's in your trousers?
Henry ⎤
         ⎟ (*together*) Yes!
Ferris ⎦
Henry So will you do it?
Ferris (*reluctantly*) Oh, all right, then.
Henry Ferris, you're a pal!

They shake hands

Ferris But it'll cost you more for late payment.
Henry How much more?
Ferris Five.
Henry Fifteen altogether?!
Ferris It's a seller's market.
Henry Go on, then—get 'em off!
Ferris Sorry?
Henry Your trousers are in Judy's bedroom.
Ferris No, no—they're *your* trousers. *These* are *my* trousers.
Henry Yes, but you're going into Judy's bathroom. That's what I'm paying you for.
Ferris But why should I have to take my trousers off?
Henry (*patiently*) When Edgar finds you in Judy's bathroom he won't expect to see you wearing trousers because he'll already have found *my* trousers in the bedroom. So go on—get 'em off!
Ferris Oh, very well... (*He starts to take off his trousers*)

Mr Johnson, seeing this happening, assumes that it is the start of an orgy, and begins to take his trousers off as well, revealing long johns. Ferris hastily stops him

No! Not you!
Johnson I thought we were going to find the ladies.
Ferris No! That's later. (*His trousers are now off*)

Disappointed, Mr Johnson pulls his trousers up again

Henry Right—give those to me.
Ferris What?
Henry Well, *your* trousers are already up there.
Ferris (*fatalistically*) And these trousers are now *your* trousers?
Ferris ⎫ (*together*) Yes!
Henry ⎭

Ferris hands over his trousers to Henry

Ferris Up the fire escape and along the little ledge?
Henry Thank you, Ferris!
Ferris I bet this sort of thing never happens to the manager of the Holiday Inn...

   Ferris goes out to the main entrance

Henry starts to put on Ferris's trousers—which are rather ill-fitting—watched by an intrigued Mr Johnson

Johnson Why are you putting on Mr Ferris's trousers?
Henry I wouldn't ask if I were you.
Johnson If we're going to find the ladies why don't you leave your trousers *off*?

Henry gives him a weary look

Henry Oh, have some more coffee! (*He refills the mug*)

   Edgar comes down the L stairs

Edgar Any sign of Ferris?
Henry (*nervously*) I think he's busy with room service.
Edgar I need to get into my wife's bathroom!
Johnson Would *you* like a cup of coffee?

Edgar glares at him

Edgar I want something stronger than coffee.

Johnson So do I…

Edgar notices Henry's ill-fitting trousers

Edgar Haven't I seen those trousers somewhere before?
Henry I'm looking after them for a friend.
Johnson Perhaps *you* know where the ladies are hiding?
Edgar What the hell do you care about ladies?

Edgar goes back up the L stairs

Henry looks closely at the potted plant

Henry That plant doesn't look too well.
Johnson I expect it needs some water.
Henry You stay here. I'm going to see how far Ferris has got on the fire
escape.

Henry goes out into the garden to check on Ferris's progress

*Mr Johnson empties his coffee into the potted plant. As he turns to go, the
plant wilts and collapses*

*Mr Johnson looks surprised, then goes off up the R stairs, smiling
optimistically*

Lights up in the Blue Room. Judy is no longer there

The door opens and Edgar bursts in and is surprised not to find her there

Edgar Judy!

The bathroom door opens and Ferris steps out, without any trousers

Ferris Help is at hand!

Edgar gazes at him in astonishment

Edgar Are you the deputy chambermaid as *well* as the deputy manager?
Ferris We're very short-staffed.
Edgar You don't seem to be staffed at all! What were you doing in there?
Ferris One of the taps was dripping.
Edgar Dripping?

Ferris Yes. It was a dripping tap. The cold one in the bath. Drip, drip, drip, it was going.

Edgar The cold one?

Ferris Drip, drip, drip. So I was fixing it.

Edgar Are you a plumber?

Ferris Drip, drip, drip...

Edgar (*louder*) Are you a plumber?

Ferris I'm a jack-of-all-trades. I can turn my hand to most things.

Edgar Yes, I bet you can...!

Ferris My sister's in Benidorm, you see...

Edgar (*impatiently*) I know that!

Ferris So that's what I was doing. Fixing the tap.

Edgar Why did you lock the bathroom door?

Ferris Have *you* ever fixed a dripping tap?

Edgar No, I don't think so...

Ferris I thought not! You don't know how hard you have to concentrate when you're doing it. The last thing you want when you're concentrating is to have people coming in and out using the facilities.

Edgar And have you fixed it now?

Ferris Sorry?

Edgar The tap! The cold tap in the bath! Have you fixed it?

Ferris There's no need to shout. Yes. I have.

Edgar Are you sure?

Ferris Well, it's not going drip, drip, drip any more.

Edgar (*thinking deeply*) Mr Ferris... there's something I don't understand...

Ferris Well, that's not surprising, is it? You've never mended a dripping tap, so of course you don't understand.

Edgar When you're mending a tap...

Ferris (*fascinated*) Yes?

Edgar Do you *always* take your trousers off?

Ferris (*laughing*) I thought you were never going to notice! (*He gives him a playful push*)

Edgar Why did you take your trousers off?

Ferris You would too if you were mending a dripping tap! I didn't want to get them wet, did I? All that water. I was standing in the bath, you see. Drip, drip, drip... You wouldn't have liked it if the deputy manager had been seen walking about with his trousers all wet, now would you?

Edgar So where *are* they?

Ferris Sorry?

Edgar Your trousers! Where are they?

Ferris They're in here, of course! I took them off in here before I went into the bathroom, didn't I?

Edgar Well, now you've finished mending the tap you'd better put them back *on* again, hadn't you?

Ferris (*confidently*) Yes—I will! (*He looks about, expecting to see the trousers, but unable to spot them. His confidence suffers a setback*) I know I put them down here *somewhere*. (*He searches, his desperation growing*)
Edgar (*watching suspiciously*) Perhaps you *hid* them under the bed?

Automatically, Ferris starts to look under the bed, then realizes that this is an unlikely scenario

Ferris Of course I didn't hide them under the bed! You are silly! (*He gives him another push*)
Edgar Then where *did* you put them?
Ferris (*his inspiration returning*) I know! The chambermaid probably thought they'd been left out to be cleaned. She's such a silly girl.
Edgar Why don't you ring her and find out? We don't want you going down stairs without your trousers on, do we?
Ferris Don't you worry. I'll find them. Anyway, you're supposed to be moving into Number Seventeen overlooking the car park. I'll be along in a minute with the menu and you won't be there.
Edgar All right, Ferris. I'll see you there in five minutes. Preferably with your trousers on!

Edgar gives Ferris a severe look, picks up his suitcase and goes

Ferris Oh, my God!

Ferris rushes into the bathroom

Lights out in the Blue Room

In the reception area, Edgar comes down the L stairs with his suitcase and goes out into the garden

Lights up in the Pink Room

The door opens slowly and Mr Johnson comes in, looking about optimistically

Angela comes out of the bathroom and sees a strange man standing in her bedroom

Angela Don't tell me you're *another* volunteer waiter?
Johnson (*with a big smile*) Oh, no—*I'm* looking for the ladies…! (*He advances hopefully, arms outstretched*)

Angela screams and runs out of the room, slamming the door behind her

Mr Johnson is disappointed by this reception and lies down under the duvet to wait

Lights out in the Pink Room

In the reception area, Angela runs down the R stairs as Henry returns from the garden. She is relieved to see him

Angela Ah! Just the man I want!

Henry is alarmed to see her approaching

Henry No! Go away! You're not to touch me! (*He tries to make his escape*)

Angela catches him and clings on desperately

Angela But there's a man in my bedroom!
Henry Yes! I know! It's your husband!
Angela No, no! Not him!
Henry *Another* man?
Angela Yes!
Henry *Two* men in your bedroom?
Angela No! Just one!
Henry What about your husband?
Angela He's gone.
Henry Thank God for that!

Angela notices he has rather short trousers

Angela Haven't I seen those trousers somewhere before?
Henry (*wearily*) It's a long story.
Angela Looks more like a *short* story. How fortunate for me that you used to be in the SAS!
Henry (*puzzled*) Sorry?
Angela You're just the man to deal with my intruder! Come along!

Angela grabs Henry's hand and drags him off up the R stairs

As they go, Judy comes down the L stairs, looking for Henry and carrying his trousers

Edgar pounds in from outside and sees her

Edgar Judy!

Judy (*jumping*) Aah! (*She sees him and quickly hides the trousers behind her back*)

Edgar You disappeared!

Judy No. *You* did.

Edgar When I came back.

Judy (*anxiously*) You came *back*?!

Edgar Yes. And you'd gone. You're hiding something!

Judy No!

Edgar You keep saying no. You've got something behind your back!

Judy No!

Edgar It's a pair of trousers!

Judy produces the trousers, sheepishly

Judy Yes...

Edgar No "no" this time? *Gentleman's* trousers!

Judy I hadn't noticed.

Edgar And I know who they belong to.

Judy Do you? Oh, dear. I can explain...!

Edgar You don't have to.

Judy Don't I?

Edgar Why are you walking about with Mr Ferris's trousers?

Judy stares at him blankly for a moment

Judy Mr Ferris's?

Edgar They're Mr Ferris's trousers!

Judy Are they?

Edgar Of course they are!

Judy (*bemused*) Oh. I didn't know that...

Edgar Why didn't the chambermaid take them?

Judy Chambermaid?

Edgar Ferris said *she*'d have taken them to the cleaners.

Judy Did he?

Edgar You're my wife!

Judy Yes—I know...!

Edgar *You* don't have to do the job of a chambermaid. I won't have a wife of mine taking the deputy manager's trousers to the cleaners.

Judy How many wives have you got?

Edgar What?!

Ferris comes down the L stairs with a bath towel wrapped around his bare legs like a sarong

Ferris! What the hell are you doing?

Ferris is frozen for a moment, then his hips start to move in a gentle Hawaiian rhythm, and he starts to sing nervously

Ferris (*singing*) "Sweet Lelani, heavenly flower, nature fashioned roses tipped with dew..."
Edgar Ferris! You're not in Hawaii now, you know!

Ferris stops his musical contribution abruptly. Edgar holds up Henry's trousers

You'd better get these back on before somebody sees you and calls the police.

Ferris glances at the trousers disparagingly

Ferris I don't want those! Where did *they* come from?
Judy (*nervously*) I found them upstairs, Mr Ferris.
Edgar Where *you* left them, remember?
Ferris (*remembering*) Ah—yes—of course! Silly of me. I'll put them on right away.

Ferris takes the trousers quickly, gives Judy a hectic look and goes into the lounge, singing as he goes

(*Singing*) "Sweet Lelani, heavenly flower..."
Edgar The sooner his sister comes back from Benidorm the better...

Edgar hastens out to the main entrance

Judy goes towards the ʟ stairs, muttering to herself

Judy If this is what having a secret sex life is like I'd sooner not bother...

Judy goes out

Lights up in the Pink Room

Angela and Henry burst in and see Mr Johnson in bed

Angela (*pointing, wildly*) There he is! He's in my *bed* now!

Mr Johnson sees Angela and smiles happily

Johnson There you are! Why did you run away from me? (*He gets out of bed, and goes towards her, his arms outstretched invitingly*)

Henry intervenes

Henry No, you don't! Come on—out! (*He pulls Mr Johnson towards the door*)
Johnson Where are we going?
Henry You can't stay in here! This isn't your room.
Johnson (*forlorn*) I haven't got a room. I'm waiting for a taxi.
Henry Well, you won't find one in here! (*He opens the door and starts to push Mr Johnson out. He looks back at Angela*) Don't worry. I'll get rid of him.
Angela You will come back?
Henry No fear!
Angela But nobody's taken my order!
Johnson *I* can do that! (*He tries to go to her*)
Henry (*restraining him*) No, you can't!
Angela (*angrily*) You said you were helping with room service!
Johnson *I* can do that! (*He tries again*)
Henry (*restraining him again*) No, you can't! (*To Angela*) Your husband will be back any minute—and I'm not climbing down that drainpipe again!

Henry bundles Mr Johnson out and goes after him, closing the door behind him

Angela sighs impatiently and goes into the bathroom

Lights out in the Pink Room

In the reception area, Henry comes down the R stairs with Mr Johnson, as Ferris comes out of the lounge. He is now wearing Henry's trousers, which do not fit him very well. He sees Mr Johnson

Ferris Where did you find *him*?
Henry In the honeymoon suite.
Ferris (*alarmed*) With Miss Forward?
Henry Yes! But don't worry. He didn't do anything.
Johnson I didn't have time...
Ferris Wasn't her husband there?
Henry No. He seems to have disappeared!
Ferris Disappeared? I haven't even *seen* him yet!
Johnson I think I'll go back upstairs... (*He makes a move for the L stairs*)

Ferris ⎫ (*together*) No!
Henry ⎭

They race after him, pick him up and bring him back as before

Ferris No, Mr Johnson! (*To Henry*) I've never known a taxi take so long to arrive. Shouldn't that pill have worn off by now?
Henry Don't ask *me*!
Ferris There's a cupboard over here. We'll put him in that until his taxi arrives.

Ferris takes Mr Johnson to the cupboard and opens the door. Mr Johnson peers inside hopefully

Johnson Is there a lady inside?
Ferris No, there isn't! That's why I'm putting *you* in there. (*He pushes him inside*)
Johnson (*looking out*) It'll be very lonely in here without a lady...

Ferris grabs a girlie magazine from the desk and thrusts it at him

Ferris There! You can look at the pictures and use your imagination! (*He closes the door and turns the key, then returns to Henry anxiously*) Was Miss Forward very angry?
Henry Well, she wasn't best pleased!
Ferris Oh, my God! She'll write an article in the Sunday paper about a dirty old man pursuing her into her boudoir!
Henry And she's getting very impatient for room service, so you'd better go and keep her sweet.
Ferris How am I going to do that?
Henry Take her some flowers! Ladies love flowers.
Ferris Do they?
Henry Of course they do, Ferris!
Ferris Oh. Right. (*He looks around and spots some rather faded flowers in a vase. He hastily takes them out of the vase and wraps them in a scruffy piece of paper*) There! How's that?

Henry looks at the flowers without enthusiasm

Henry How could she resist them? Any chance of food, Ferris? I seem to have worked up quite an appetite.
Ferris How can you think of food in the middle of a crisis?

Ferris hastens out up the R stairs with his bunch of flowers

Henry goes into the kitchen, searching for food

Lights up in the Pink Room. A knock at the door

Angela comes out of the bathroom as Ferris arrives with the bunch of flowers

Angela Oh, Francis ... you brought me flowers... (*She takes them with as much enthusiasm as she can muster*)
Ferris (*modestly*) Just a small bunch...
Angela A little limp.
Ferris Sorry?
Angela But it's the thought that counts.

Ferris glances about nervously

Ferris No sign of your husband?
Angela You don't have to worry. He won't be coming back. So we're all alone... (*She gazes at the flowers*) Fancy you bringing me flowers, Francis...
Ferris Ah—yes—well, there was a good reason for that...

Angela casts the flowers aside on to the bed and closes to him

Angela Yes. I know, Francis. You're a very understanding man and you know what I want, don't you?
Ferris I'm not here for that!
Angela Then why have you brought me flowers?
Ferris (*stammering*) Th-th-th-th-they're a peace offering!
Angela Peace offering, Francis? I didn't know that we'd been fighting. (*She closes to him again*)

Ferris escapes a little

Ferris To apologise for the unexpected visitor you had just now!
Angela You mean the *old* gentleman?
Ferris Yes. It must have been such a nasty shock for you.
Angela Oh, you mustn't worry, Francis. The SAS man soon got rid of him.
Ferris My sister and I wouldn't like you to think that we allow dirty old men like that to invade the privacy of unaccompanied ladies. It's not hotel policy, you understand?

Angela sits on the bed invitingly

Angela Why don't you come and sit over here? (*She pats the bed beside her*)
Ferris (*trying to ignore her invitation*) I wouldn't like you to write about such
  things in the newspaper.
Angela (*puzzled*) Sorry?
Ferris In your article—in the Sunday newspaper—about this hotel. It
  wouldn't be good for business.
Angela Francis, what *are* you talking about?

Ferris begins to have doubts

Ferris That *is* what you're here for, isn't it? To write about my sister's hotel
  in your column?
Angela (*laughing*) Good heavens, no! Whatever gave you that idea?

*Ferris freezes for a moment as this information sinks in. Then he activates
himself wildly*

Ferris But I—I put you in this room specially because—you—you mean it
  isn't you? You mean you're *not* a journalist?
Angela No! Of course I'm not!
Ferris (*appalled*) Oh, my God! Then it must be somebody else! (*He grabs
  her hand and pulls her abruptly to her feet, abandoning his sycophancy at
  once*) You can't stay in here!
Angela But this is where you put me.
Ferris It was a mistake!
Angela Francis?
Ferris Quick! Pack your things! You're leaving!

   *Ferris starts to go, then remembers his bunch of flowers, rushes back to
   collect them, and runs out, closing the door behind him*

Bewildered, Angela starts to pack her case

   *In the reception area, Ferris runs down the R stairs and casts the flowers
   aside as Henry comes out of the kitchen, eating a sandwich*

It's the wrong one!

Puzzled, Henry looks at his sandwich

Henry It's ham. (*He holds it up for inspection*)
Ferris The one up there with the second husband!
Henry Miss Forward?

Ferris Yes! She's not the one! You told me she was the one, and she's not!
Henry Not what?
Ferris The person who writes about hotels! It's not her! And if it's not her who the hell is it?
Henry But, Ferris—nobody else has arrived.
Ferris (*suddenly realizing*) Ah—yes—they have!
Henry Have they?
Ferris Your lady friend's husband! *He* arrived!
Henry Edgar?
Ferris Yes! *He* turned up here unexpectedly! So it must be him! (*He starts to go, then hesitates*) Get my trousers off! I want them back. Oh, my God...!

Ferris races off up the R *stairs*

Bemused, Henry starts to take off Ferris's trousers

In the Pink Room, Angela has finished packing as Ferris runs in and grabs her abruptly

Right! Come on! Don't hang about!
Angela Where am I going?
Ferris Back to your old room!
Angela But I prefer this one.
Ferris Well, you can't have it!

Ferris drags Angela out with her bag

Lights out in the Pink Room

In the reception area, Henry finishes taking off his trousers as Ferris and Angela arrive

Angela is surprised to see Henry without any trousers

(*To Angela*) You stay here!

Ferris grabs the trousers from Henry and runs out up the L *stairs*

Angela (*intrigued*) Why have you taken your trousers off?
Henry Because Ferris asked me to.
Angela Do you always take your trousers off when a hotel manager asks you to?

Henry It was an emergency.
Angela But why did you give them to Francis?
Henry Because they belong to him! I just borrowed them.
Angela You borrowed Francis's trousers?
Henry Yes!
Angela Do you often go around borrowing other people's trousers?
Henry I had no choice!
Angela And what have you done with your *own* trousers?
Henry (*impatiently*) I lent them to Francis, of course!

Angela tries to understand this sartorial arrangement. Lights up in the Blue Room

Ferris races in breathlessly, as Judy comes out of the bathroom. He is now back in his own trousers and carrying Henry's. He grabs Judy's hand

Judy (*outraged*) Mr Ferris! What's your game?
Ferris You can't stay in here!
Judy But you put me in here.
Ferris It was a mistake! Come along!

Ferris drags Judy out, closing the door behind them

Lights out in the Blue Room

Henry Oh, my God...!
Angela Whatever's the matter?
Henry I'm standing here talking to you without my trousers on! If Edgar comes in and finds me talking to you without my trousers on he'll kill me!

Ferris arrives with Judy. He sits her on the sofa abruptly

Ferris Stay there! I'll be back in a minute. (*He throws the trousers to Henry*)

Henry catches them

Judy (*seeing him*) Oh, *there* you are, Henry!

Ferris grabs Angela's hand

Ferris Right! You're coming with me! (*He pulls her towards the L stairs*)
Judy How did you get out of the bathroom?
Angela (*calling as she goes*) He used to be in the SAS!

Ferris and Angela go out up the L stairs at speed

Judy I wish I knew what was going on. What on earth was Mr Ferris doing with your trousers?
Henry You'd never believe me if I told you.

Edgar comes in from the garden and sees Henry without his trousers

Edgar What the hell are you doing taking your trousers off in front of my wife?
Judy Oh, Edgar! He wasn't taking them off, he was putting them on.
Edgar I can't think why he took them off in the first place!
Judy (*quietly*) *I* can…! (*She grins at Henry*)

They freeze as…

Lights up in the Blue Room

Ferris arrives with Angela and pushes her into the room unceremoniously

Ferris There you are—back where you belong! (*He tries to leave*)
Angela (*coldly*) Shall I be *staying* here this time?
Ferris Yes! (*He moves again*)
Angela You won't be moving me out again?
Ferris No! (*He moves again*)
Angela Then you'd better fetch more gin.
Ferris More gin. Right! (*He moves again*)
Angela On the house.
Ferris On the house? (*Seeing her about to insist*) Right! (*He moves again*)
Angela And tonic.
Ferris And tonic. Right! (*He moves again*)
Angela And lemon!
Ferris (*without stopping this time*) And lemon! Right!

Ferris darts out, closing the door behind him

Angela sighs and goes into the bathroom as the Lights go out in the Blue Room

In the reception area, Edgar is glaring at Henry, who is putting his trousers on

Edgar If I catch you taking your trousers off in front of my wife again you know what'll happen?

Henry I can guess...!

A sudden knocking inside the cupboard. They react

Judy (*puzzled*) There's someone in the cupboard!
Henry It's all right. He's got a magazine to look at.

Judy and Edgar are surprised

> *Ferris comes down the L stairs, sees Edgar and goes to him, eager to ingratiate himself*

Ferris Ah! There you are, sir! I've been looking for you.
Edgar You didn't look far.
Ferris You won't be sleeping over the car park after all!
Edgar I won't?
Ferris I've got a *special* room for you, sir!
Edgar You have?
Ferris (*bowing low*) A special room for a special person...
Edgar Have you gone mad, Ferris?
Ferris This way, sir! (*He leads the way to the R stairs*)
Edgar Oh, very well. If you insist. (*He joins Ferris*)
Ferris After *you*, sir! (*Another gracious bow*)

> *Puzzled, Edgar goes up the R stairs, followed by Ferris*

Judy Why is Mr Ferris being so nice to Edgar?
Henry I think he thinks he's someone else.
Judy I wish he *was*...!

They laugh

> Henry ... do you think we could forget about sex now and talk about food? I'm starving!
Henry Then you come with me! I've made friends with the chef.

They start to go

Judy I'll say *one* thing for you, Henry.
Henry Oh?
Judy You're better at putting your trousers *on* than you are at taking them *off*!

Henry and Judy laugh and go into the kitchen

Lights up in the Pink Room

Ferris comes in, smiling enthusiastically, followed by Edgar

Ferris There we are, sir! This is much more suitable for you. The honeymoon suite!

Edgar recognizes the room with alarm

Edgar You're not putting me in here with Angela!
Ferris Oh, no, sir! This room is specially for *you*—all on your own.
Edgar But this room's already occupied!
Ferris No, no!
Edgar Yes, yes! I'm not staying here! I prefer the room over the car park. (*He starts to go*)

Ferris pursues him in a high state and brings him back as he babbles on

Ferris But this is the best room in the hotel! That's why I brought you here. You'll like it, I know you will! Let me get you a drink, sir. Champagne? Whisky-and-soda? What's your particular preference? You only have to say the word. Smoked salmon? Caviar? All on the house! Your wish is our command!
Edgar What's the matter with you, Ferris? Have you gone mad? Why all this VIP treatment all of a sudden?
Ferris Oh ... you know, sir! (*He grins and nudges him playfully*)
Edgar No, I do *not* know!
Ferris (*confidentially*) My sister would want you to write about the *best* room in the hotel, now wouldn't she, sir?
Edgar Why should I want to write to anybody about *this* dump? I only came here because the other hotels were full.

Ferris accepts this body blow with as much fortitude as he can muster

Ferris But isn't that what you're here for? To write an article for a Sunday newspaper?
Edgar Write an article? Don't be daft! I'm in the building trade. And I don't like the look of this room one bit. It's far too pink. I'm going back to my room over the car park!

Edgar storms out

Ferris dithers, desperately

Ferris Oh, my God...!

Ferris runs out after Edgar

Lights out in the Pink Room

In the reception area, Edgar comes down the R stairs, with Ferris fluttering along in his wake, as Henry and Judy come out of the kitchen. She is eating a sandwich. Edgar sees them and is immediately suspicious

Edgar What were you doing with my wife in the kitchen?
Henry Getting her a sandwich. The poor woman was starving.
Edgar Well, at least you had your trousers on this time! (*He joins Judy*)
Henry (*going to Ferris*) Didn't he approve of the honeymoon suite?
Ferris No! He didn't! And he *isn't*!
Henry Isn't?
Ferris What we thought he was!

Angela comes angrily down the L stairs

Angela Ferris! You never brought me my gin!
Ferris No. I had other things on my mind...!

Angela sees Edgar. And Edgar sees her, and shrinks, fearful of the revelation that now seems imminent

Angela Oh. *You*'re still here, then?
Judy (*surprised*) Have you two met?
Edgar No!
Angela Yes, we have!
Ferris Yes, they have! They're old friends.
Judy Edgar, you never told me that you'd run into an old friend.
Edgar D-didn't I?
Angela (*puzzled*) Why are you calling him Edgar? Do *you* know him as well?
Judy Know him? I should say so! He's my husband.
Angela He *can't* be!
Judy Well, he *is*!
Angela But Edgar happens to be *my* husband!

They all react

Ferris (*aside, to Henry*) I thought there were *two* husbands.
Henry (*aside, to Ferris*) So did I. And I've been running away from *both* of them!

Judy (*to Angela*) *Your* husband?

Angela Yes.

Judy Edgar? It's not true, is it? You're married to me. You can't be married to this lady as well.

Edgar (*a beaten man*) I'm afraid I am...

Judy You mean you've got *two* wives?

Edgar Yes...

Judy You dirty old man!

Edgar But I haven't seen this one for years! (*He indicates Angela*)

Ferris (*to Henry*) I think I've lost track of the conversation. (*He goes to Edgar*) Let's get this straight. You're married to *both* these ladies?

Edgar Yes..

Ferris Both at the same time?

Edgar (*defensively*) There were a few years in between!

Angela And he hasn't seen me for ages.

Judy But you're still married to him?

Angela Yes...

Ferris Wait a minute! You mean you never got divorced from *this* one before you got married to *this* one?

Edgar No...

Ferris In that case you can't really be married to *this* one! (*He indicates Judy*)

Judy That *is* a relief...!

Henry Is that true, Ferris?

Ferris Of course it's true! He's still married to Miss Forward.

Henry (*to Judy*) So that's all right, then, isn't it?

Judy Is it?

Henry If you're not really married at all *we* may as well move back into the honeymoon suite.

Judy (*smiling happily*) Oh, Henry, what a good idea! Then I can help you take off your trousers again.

Edgar (*furiously*) You wouldn't dare!

Henry ⎫ (*together*) Yes, we would!
Judy ⎭

Edgar Ferris...?

Ferris Yes, they would!

Henry and Judy go towards the R *stairs, his arm around her*

Edgar I'll kill him!

Ferris I don't think he's bothered. Are you, Henry?

Henry No. *I'm* only frightened of *husbands*!

Henry and Judy go, smiling happily, up the R *stairs*

Angela goes to Edgar

Angela *You*'d better come with *me*, then, Edgar.
Edgar (*surprised*) Do you want me to?
Angela No, but I don't have much choice, do I? (*She smiles at him, fondly*)
Oh, come on. Edgar! After all, you are still married to me.

They go towards the L stairs, then she looks back at Ferris

I never thought I'd come here and end up in bed with my own husband!

Angela and Edgar go

From outside we hear a car horn blasting impatiently. Ferris reacts

Ferris Ah! That'll be the taxi! (*He realizes*) Oh, my God! I'd forgotten all
about him! (*He races across to the cupboard, unlocks it and opens the
door*)

Mr Johnson comes out. He has now lost his libido and is back to normal

Johnson I've been having such a lovely sleep...
Ferris Well, your taxi's here now so you can be on your way. (*He goes to
pick up Mr Johnson's suitcase*)
Johnson I dreamt I was in a lady's boudoir...
Ferris That wasn't a dream!
Johnson (*taking his case*) Mr Ferris, I wonder if you could do me a favour?
Ferris Depends what it is.
Johnson Could you let me have some more of those indigestion tablets?
Ferris No, I couldn't! (*He urges Mr Johnson on his way*)
Johnson Not even if I promise not to mention them in my article?
Ferris (*frozen*) What?
Johnson In my article for the Sunday newspaper.
Ferris Oh, no! It—it isn't *you*?
Johnson Oh, yes. I've been writing that column for years and years.
Ferris Oh, my God...!
Johnson And just think of it—people in and out of bedrooms, men
exchanging trousers, guests being locked in cupboards. It's going to make
very interesting reading...

*Mr Johnson smiles serenely and goes out to the main entrance with his
suitcase*

Ferris panics

Ferris No! Wait a minute! Mr Johnson! (*He quickly gets the packet of pills from the desk and races after Mr Johnson*) Wait! You've forgotten your indigestion tablets! Mr Johnson...!

Music plays as Ferris disappears after Mr Johnson in a high state of alarm as——

——the CURTAIN *falls*

FURNITURE AND PROPERTY LIST

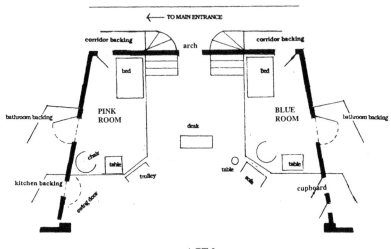

ACT I

On stage: RECEPTION:
Reception desk. *On it:* bell, phone, register, menu, dish of chocolates.
In drawer: "No Vacancies" sign, "girlie" magazine, pills, old
newspaper
Drinks trolley. *On it:* bottle of gin, small bottles of tonic, glasses,
opener, small tray, jug of water, slices of lemon on sticks
Small dilapidated sofa. *On it:* newspaper
Potted plant (collapsible) on tray
Small table. *On it:* faded flowers in vase
Small cupboard (lockable)

PINK ROOM:
Four-poster bed with bedding
Table. *On it:* phone
Small armchair

BLUE ROOM:
Bed. *On it:* bedding; open, half-packed suitcase; other clothing,
including men's pyjamas
Small armchair
Table. *On it:* phone, vase of flowers

Off stage: Weekend bag containing clothes and frilly night-dress (**Angela**)
Tray with bottle of champagne and two flutes (**Ferris**)
Weekend bag (**Judy**)
Small suitcase (**Edgar**)
Overnight bag (**Henry**)

Personal: **Henry:** money
Ferris: wrist-watch (worn throughout)

ACT II

On stage: As before

Off stage: Pot of coffee, mug (**Ferris**)
Suitcase (**Edgar**)
Henry's trousers (**Judy**)
Sandwich (**Henry**)
Henry's trousers (**Ferris**)
Sandwich (**Judy**)

Personal: **Edgar:** money

LIGHTING PLOT

Property fittings required: nil
1 interior. The same throughout

ACT I

To open: General lighting in reception

ACT II

Cue 24	**Henry**: """What?!"""	(Page 56)
	Lights out in Pink Room	
Cue 25	**Edgar** goes up R stairs	(Page 58)
	Lights up in Pink Room	
Cue 26	**Edgar**: "…I must talk to you about…!"	(Page 61)
	Lights out in Pink Room	
Cue 27	**Ferris** hastens into kitchen	(Page 65)
	Lights up in Pink Room	
Cue 28	**Angela** goes into bathroom	(Page 66)
	Lights out in Pink Room	
Cue 29	**Edgar** goes into lounge	(Page 66)
	Lights up in Blue Room	
Cue 30	**Judy** and **Henry** sit on end of bed	(Page 67)
	Lights out in Blue Room	
Cue 31	**Mr Johnson** goes out after **Ferris**	(Page 70)
	Lights up in Blue Room	
Cue 32	**Judy** starts to go	(Page 74)
	Lights out in Blue Room	
Cue 33	**Mr Johnson** goes up R stairs	(Page 79)
	Lights up in Blue Room	
Cue 34	**Ferris** rushes into bathroom	(Page 81)
	Lights out in Blue Room	
Cue 35	**Edgar** goes out into garden	(Page 81)
	Lights up in Pink Room	
Cue 36	**Mr Johnson** lies down under duvet	(Page 82)
	Lights out in Pink Room	
Cue 37	**Judy** goes out	(Page 84)
	Lights up in Pink Room	
Cue 38	**Angela** goes into bathroom	(Page 85)
	Lights out in Pink Room	

EFFECTS PLOT

ACT I

Cue 1   To open Act I   (Page 1)
Music until lights come up in reception area

Cue 2   After long silence, **Ferris** asleep   (Page 1)
Reception phone rings loudly

Cue 3   **Angela**: "…isn't good enough, is it?"   (Page 24)
Music until **Ferris** *enters Blue Room*

Cue 4   **Henry**: "That was a compliment, wasn't it?"   (Page 41)
Reception phone rings loudly

ACT II

Cue 5   To open Act II   (Page 46)
Music until lights come up in reception area

Cue 6   **Ferris**: "She and Edgar are already in it."   (Page 47)
Reception phone rings loudly

Cue 7   **Angela**: "Yes."   (Page 60)
Noise of window banging shut in bathroom

Cue 8   **Edgar**: "Overlooking the car park."   (Page 73)
Noise inside bathroom

Cue 9   **Angela** and **Edgar** exit   (Page 96)
Impatient car horn outside

Cue 10   **Ferris** pursues **Mr Johnson**   (Page 97)
Music, continuing throughout curtain calls

Lightning Source UK Ltd.
Milton Keynes UK
UKHW021254250822
407831UK00014B/177

9 780573 019937